Time for HOMEWORK

Colleen Timoshenko

5

Book 5

Hunter Education Nightingale

HUNTER
EDUCATION
NIGHTINGALE

Time for Homework - Book 5

Published by:
Hunter Education Nightingale
ABN: 69 055 798 626
PO Box 547
Warners Bay NSW 2282
email: sales@huntereducationnightingale.com.au
paul@huntereducationnightingale.com.au
www.huntereducationnightingale.com.au

Cover Design: Doriana Berkovic

National Library of Australia Card No.
and ISBN 978 - 1 - 922242 - 29 - 7

F E D C B A
21 20 19 18 17 16

Time for Homework
Book 5

About this Book

Time for Homework Book 5 is the sixth in a series of seven books written to help reinforce many of the concepts, skills and understanding needed for today's school curriculum.

The series is designed as a user-friendly resource to improve a student's reading skills, knowledge of grammar, accuracy in spelling and improved word knowledge through word building activities. Questions covering the New Mathematics Curriculum complete each unit.

The book contains 30 units of work and one unit can be attempted each week. Each unit addresses the subjects outlined above and covers topics in today's environment which are relevant to the new Australian Curriculum for English and Mathematics.

As the child gains a better knowledge of language; reading, interpreting and responding to the written text develops and improves. Knowledge of grammar, punctuation and spelling, as well as mathematics is acquired by completing the set activities.

While *Time for Homework* treats many of the topics presented in the school curriculum, it is a summary only of those subjects. This book is fun to use at home, with the child, as a resource, to develop and improve learning.

Message to Parents

With *Time for Homework, Book 5*, your child should not need help with reading or the explanation of instructions. As a parent you are asked to support your child's learning but resist the temptation to provide answers. By all means, read a word for your child if necessary and then support him/her to gain a better knowledge about the word and its meaning. This reassures the child and enables one to become a more independent learner. As the child works through the book your encouragement may be all that is needed.

Regular homework helps your child develop skills which will assist in the learning process and improve confidence over time. A confident and skilled learner will enjoy school.

Praise your child at all times because you are the ideal support person in your child's life. Use this book together to make the learning process more meaningful for both of you.

Time for Homework, Book 5 is designed as a fun book for home use. Enjoy the journey!

Narrative

Smithton's Surfing Spectacular

"Not long to wait now for the big day!" cried Sam.

"I get more excited every time I ride these waves!" Patrick squealed.

The up-coming event was the one they looked forward to during the long, summer school holidays. They would hang out with their mates and practise from early morning until they started to feel hungry. When the surf was up they made the most of it, just to be ready to compete in the Annual Surf Spectacular.

Because school had to take first priority now, it was only possible to meet up for a surf before breakfast and then in the late afternoon. There was no guarantee the breakers would be suitable to test the limits of the competitors. Then again, there was no guarantee the surf would be any good at all! In past years, some of the events could not go ahead as planned, because the ocean was either too flat or too treacherous. Just being its cantankerous self; deciding to show everyone what mother- nature was capable of producing and spoiling everyone's expectations for the big day of junior competition.

Everything depended on the weather and at this time of the year it could be unsettled for days. All the boys could do was practice and wait.

Understanding

Use the narrative to answer each question.

a. What was Sam waiting for? ______

b. In the holidays, when did the boys practice? ______

c. What got in the way of surfing all day? ______

d. Why could practise be disrupted? ______

e. Who in the reading is identified as "its cantankerous self"? ______

f. Where does this event take place? ______

Interpreting

Circle **T** (true) or **F** (false) to answer correctly.

a. These events are held each year.	**T**	**F**
b. There are events for all ages in the competition.	**T**	**F**
c. Sam gets excited just waiting to ride the waves.	**T**	**F**
d. There are only two boys practising for the competition.	**T**	**F**
e. The ocean can be unpredictable and spoil everything.	**T**	**F**
f. The best thing to do is be prepared for anything.	**T**	**F**

Grammar

Find the adjectives that describe each noun in the narrative and write them on the line.

a. ______, ______, ______ holidays.

b. ______, ______, Spectacular.

c. ______ self

d. ______ day and ______ competition.

e. ______ morning. **f.** ______ years.

Spelling

Unit 1

Spelling Rule: Words with a consonant followed by **'y'**, change the **'y'** to **'I'** before adding **'ed'**. Add **'ed'** to each word:

a. hurry __________ **b.** try __________

c. terrify __________ **d.** study __________

Syllabification: Write each word in syllables. (*Each syllable has a vowel sound.*)

a. spectacular __________

b. squealed __________

c. guarantee __________ **d.** treacherous __________

e. cantankerous __________ **f.** expectations __________

Word Building

Add the suffixes **'ed'** and **'ing'** to each word.

a. cry __________ __________

b. compete __________ __________

c. return __________ __________

Punctuation

Capital letters are used: to begin sentences, for proper nouns and for titles.

Re-write each sentence using capital letters where needed.

a. phil and john went to the sunday matinee.

____

b. the boys joined the bears football team together.

____

c. in february, the prime minister, mrs albright, visited our school.

____

Place Value

1. Write the number represented on each place value card.

a.

TTH	TH	H	T	O
III	IIII	I	IIIII	IIIII

____

b.

TTH	TH	H	T	O
I	III	IIIII	IIIIII	III

____

c.

TTH	TH	H	T	O
IIIIIII		IIIIII	IIIIIII	III

____

2. Write the place value for each circled number.

a. 8 (3) 2 4 1 __________

b. 7 5 (1) 6 7 __________

c. 3 (8) 5 2 9 __________

3. Write the whole number for each expanded number.

a. 60 000+4 000+200+70+6= __________

b. 70 000+2 000+900+40+2= __________

c. 30 000+8 000+700+50+1= __________

Addition

1. Add each group of numbers to find the total.

a. 27 + 42 + 38 =

b. 46 + 38 + 24 =

c. 143 + 27 + 19 =

d. 244 + 38 + 56 =

2. Add the four-digit numbers using trading with tens and ones.

a.

	TH	H	T	O
	6	3	2	6
+	2	3	3	9

b.

	TH	H	T	O
	4	1	7	8
+	3	5	1	7

c.

	TH	H	T	O
	1	3	7	6
+	5	3	1	6

d.

	TH	H	T	O
	5	1	6	5
+	3	2	7	8

The Tropical Rainforest

Information Report

A rainforest can be hot and steamy resembling an enormous greenhouse. Mostly, a rainforest has a temperature around 26°C with an average rainfall of 150 cm each year.

The hot, humid climate of a rainforest means trees and plants grow very quickly. Huge tree canopies prevent the sunlight from reaching the forest floor. Vegetation usually grows low and tangled forming a thick, green cover on the ground. Flowers and plants, that like the temperature in the rainforest, usually grow quite large.

There are many layers to a rainforest. There are also many animals living in the shrubs and trees. Birds and butterflies, frogs and lizards even monkeys and bats frequent different layers of the forest. Many of these animals are very rare and cannot be found anywhere else in the World. Most of the animals are found on the canopy layer where food is plentiful. Trees that break through to the sunlight often grow to 40m. Large birds, such as eagles, can be seen searching for food in these tall trees.

Vegetation on the rainforest floor creates a suitable home for many forest critters. The trees that fell during wind storms and heavy rain, which weakens their roots, provide suitable accommodation for small, furry creatures to live in and breed. These habitats provide several generations of forest animals with the safety and security they need to grow and regenerate away from the more dangerous creatures of the forest.

Understanding

Tick the box if the information is in the text

a. Rainforests are cold, humid places. ☐

b. Rainforests are like big hothouses. ☐

c. Plants grow quite slowly in rainforests. ☐

d. Huge tree-tops cover forest floors. ☐

e. Many rare animals live in rainforests. ☐

f. Eagles fly across the 40m tree-tops. ☐

g. Large plants grow on rainforest floors. ☐

h. A rainforest has very little rain each year. ☐

i. Animal habitats are safe and secure. ☐

j. Wind and rain causes rainforest trees to fall. ☐

Interpreting

Match a word to its meaning

WORD BANK: resembling, average, canopy, vegetation, plentiful, tropical

a. local plant life ____________________

b. a typical amount, quantity ____________________

c. within the tropics ____________________

d. similar likeness ____________________

e. in abundance ____________________

f. overhead covering ____________________

Grammar

Write the **adjective** used to describe the noun.

a. ____________________ greenhouse

b. ____________________ rainfall

c. ______________, ______________ climate

d. ____________________ animals

e. The Tropical Rainforest is an ____________________ Report.

f. ______________, ______________ creatures live in the rainforest..

Spelling

Homophones - Words that sound the same with a different meaning and spelling.
Match each word to its correct meaning. - **rain, reign, rein**

a. a period of rule by a monarch. ____________

b. water from the sky ____________

c. a strap for guiding a horse ____________

Syllabification: Write each word in syllables.

a. tropical ____________

b. enormous ____________ **c.** canopies ____________

d. different ____________ **e.** rainforest ____________

f. plentiful ____________

Word Building

Use blends and endings to make new words.
Make words ending in **'ead'** using these blends.

a. spr ____________ **b.** thr ____________

c. dr ____________

Make words ending in **'end'** using these blends.

a. sp ____________ **b.** tr ____________

c. bl ____________

Punctuation

Use capital letters for titles and to show respect.

Write each title or organisation's name using capital letters correctly.

a. the junior red cross

____

b. her majesty, queen elizabeth

____

c. the royal australian air force

____

d. the honourable judge john dew

____

Subtraction

1. Find the difference without trading, for these numbers.

a. 725 - 312 = ☐

b. 869 - 314 = ☐

c. 657 - 223 = ☐

d. 489 - 267 = ☐

2. Find the difference using trading, with tens and ones.

a.

	TH	H	T	O
	8	3	5	4
–	5	1	2	7

b.

	TH	H	T	O
	7	8	7	3
–	2	1	4	8

c.

	TH	H	T	O
	8	5	7	2
–	3	3	1	9

d.

	TH	H	T	O
	6	9	5	0
–	4	3	1	4

Multiplication

1. Write each multiplication number sentence as an algorithm.

a. 1 232 x 2 =

TH	H	T	O
X			

b. 3 122 x 3 =

TH	H	T	O
X			

c. 1 222 x 4 =

TH	H	T	O
X			

2.

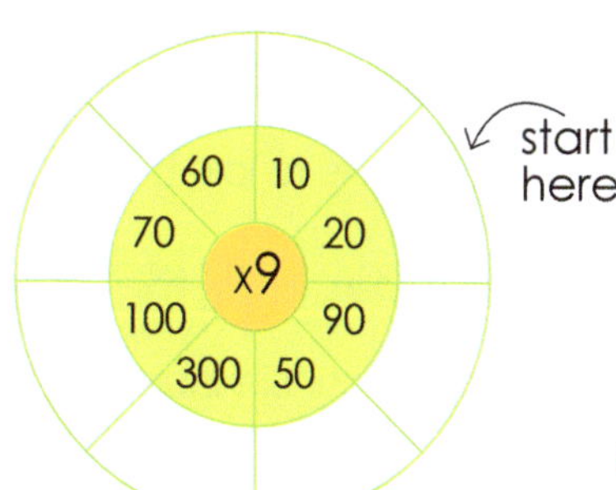

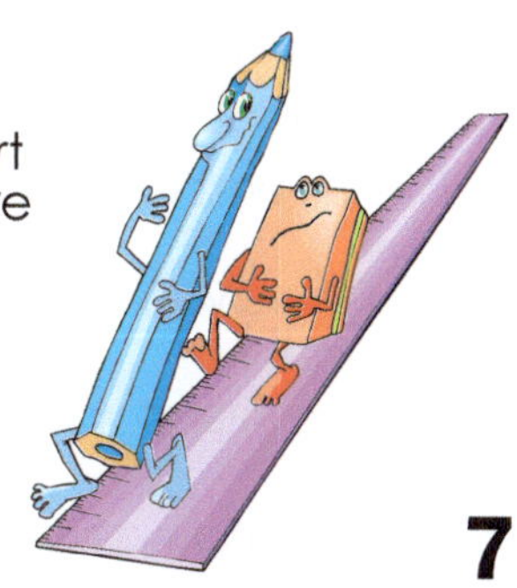

At the beginning of the 20th Century travel to distant places in the World was on newly built ocean liners. Shipping companies were building luxury passenger liners capable of accommodating travellers in large numbers. The Cunard Line was one such company. It built its luxury liner, the Titanic, between 1909 and 1911 and declared her 'unsinkable' because of her design.

Rich people sailed across the oceans for pleasure en route to other continents. Others, who were intent on beginning a new life in North America, away from the poverty and famine gripping their own homeland, also undertook these journeys. The Titanic's manifest identified a combination of both rich and poor with the poor berthed in the lower sections of the vessel. Many poor families embarked on the Titanic when she called into Irish ports after sailing from Southhampton, in England, to New York in USA on 12 April 1912.

On the evening of 15 April, 1912, while the ship was in the North Sea, steaming towards New York, she collided with a submerged iceberg. This cut a hole in the hull causing her to take in water and sink. There were over 2 200 people on board that fateful night and only enough life boats to hold 1 200 of them. Panic set in when this failure was discovered and many people jumped overboard and drowned. Others just stayed on board the ship after the last of the lifeboats were lowered into the water. Over 1 500 people died when the Titanic sank that night.

Understanding

Shade the bubble for the best

a. These events happened
- ◯ in the 1700s
- ◯ in the 1800s
- ◯ in the 1900s
- ◯ in the 2000s

b. The Titanic was
- ◯ a luxury liner
- ◯ unsinkable
- ◯ only for the rich people
- ◯ on its way to England

c. Passengers on the Titanic were
- ◯ mainly rich Englishmen
- ◯ mainly poor Americans
- ◯ mainly poor Irish
- ◯ mainly rich some poor

d. Survivors of the Titanic numbered about
- ◯ 700
- ◯ 1 200
- ◯ 1 500
- ◯ 2 200

Interpreting

Write an answer to each question

a. Where were the Titanic's last ports of call? ____________________

b. From where did the ship sail and where was it going? ____________________

c. How long had the ship been at sea before the disaster? ____________________

d. What caused the disaster? ____________________

e. Why were so few lives saved? ____________________

Grammar

Use **Conjunctions** to join sentences. **and, but or so**

Write the best conjunction on the line to join both sentences.

a. There was a famine in Ireland. Many people left for other parts of the World. __________

b. The Titanic was thought to be unsinkable. This was not the case. __________

c. The ship was sailing in the North Sea. The iceberg cut a hole in its side. __________

Spelling

Silent letters to begin words. Silent "W"

write, wreck, wrong, wrap, wrinkle, writhe, wring, wrath, wrestle

Say each word and then match it to its meaning.

a. incorrect ____________ **b.** to damage ____________

c. to compose ____________ **d.** to crease ____________

e. to cover ____________ **f.** to twist and turn ____________

g. to grapple ____________ **h.** fierce anger ____________

i. to force out moisture ____________

Word Building

Use blends and endings to make new words.
Make words ending in **'ear'** using these blends.

a. cl ____________

b. sh ____________

c. sp ____________

d. sm ____________

Syllabification: Write each word in syllables.

a. beginning ____________ **b.** accommodating ____________

c. unsinkable ____________ **d.** submerged ____________

e. collided ____________ **f.** discovered ____________

Punctuation

Question Mark? or Exclamation Mark!

Mark each sentence with the correct punctuation mark.

a. How did you do that **b.** Wow **c.** What's the date today

d. "How wonderful " I cried. **e.** Is it raining **f.** Well done Sue

g. How many were saved **h.** Jump **i.** Why did he leave early

Prime Numbers

1. Write the factors for each number.

a. 12 ____, ____, ____, ____, ____, ____

b. 15 ____, ____, ____, ____,

c. 20 ____, ____, ____, ____, ____, ____

d 39 ____, ____, ____, ____

2. Answer True (T) or False (F) to these.

a. 8 is a factor of 24 ________

b. 27 is a factor of 81 ________

c. 17 is a factor of 51 ________

d. 7 is a factor of 27 ________

3. Colour the multiples for each number.

a.

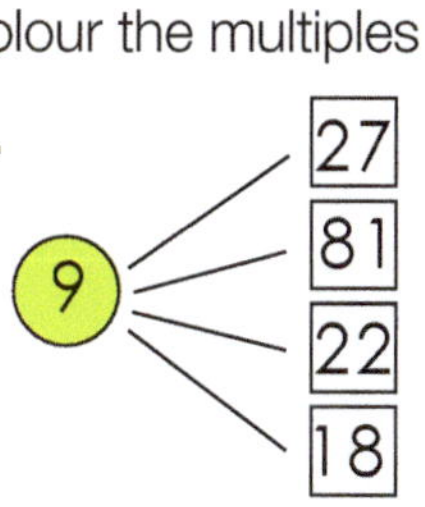

b.

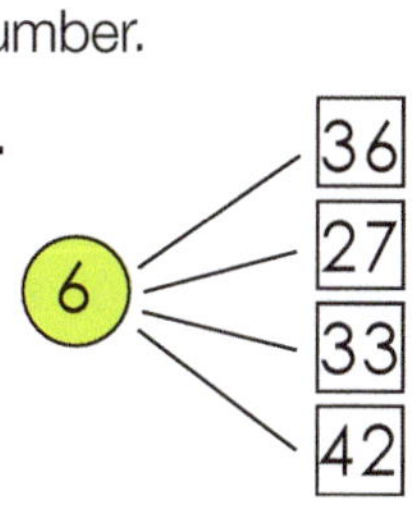

Multiplication

1. Convert each number sentence to a formal operation and then write the answer.

a. $30 \div 3 =$ ☐ **b.** $27 \div 3 =$ ☐

c. $48 \div 6 =$ ☐ **d.** $32 \div 4 =$ ☐

2. Write the improper fraction as a completed number sentence.

a. $\frac{28}{4} =$ ☐ $\div$ ☐ $=$ ☐

b. $\frac{39}{3} =$ ☐ $\div$ ☐ $=$ ☐

c. $\frac{24}{6} =$ ☐ $\div$ ☐ $=$ ☐

Visual Text

Summer Weather Patterns in Australia

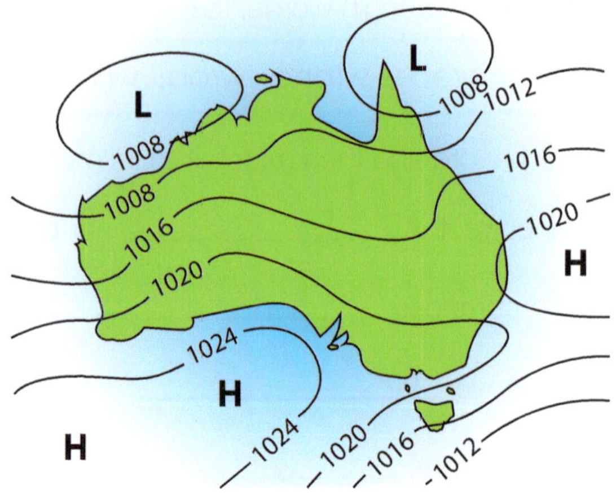

What are weather patterns and where are they found? How are they read and what do they mean?
The lines on the map of Australia show weather patterns of highs and lows which indicate hot dry weather or cold, moist air moving around the country. During the summer, high pressure systems move from west to east across the Southern Ocean and Great Australian Bight. These systems bring hot, dry winds followed by cooler, southerly changes which are often called 'southerly busters' in the east or the 'Freemantle Doctor' in Perth.
When low pressure cells form in the northern and eastern part of Australia they bring summer rains that often cause minor flooding on the east coast. In the northern tropics this season is called 'the wet' and creates havoc and isolation, with properties often cut off for many weeks during the seasonal wet. Also, during the summer months, tropical cyclones form in the waters off the Australian coast in either the west or the east. These tropical cyclones are given female names which are chosen from a letter of the alphabet. The last cyclone of the season could be called Cyclone Mary so the first of the next season would be given a female name starting with 'N'.

Understanding

Tick the box if you can find this information in the text.

Summer weather patterns

- **a.** are lines on a map ☐
- **b.** tell of hot, dry weather ☐
- **c.** show how air moves around ☐
- **d.** identify high and low pressure systems ☐
- **e.** show highs bringing hot, dry winds ☐
- **f.** show lows that can bring very wet weather ☐
- **g.** show wind movements from west to east ☐
- **h.** identify tropical cyclones in warm, coastal waters ☐

Interpreting

Write an answer to each question

a. What are cool, southerly changes often called in eastern Australia?____________________

b. What happens in 'the wet'? ____________________

c. In Australia, where would you be in 'the wet'? ____________________

d. Write the name of the months during which tropical cyclones occur?____________________

e. Colour the potential cyclones showing on the above map of Australia.

Grammar

Underline the common nouns in red and the proper nouns in blue in each sentence.

a. The map of Australia shows high and low pressure system weather patterns.

b. In summer, highs move east from the Southern Ocean and the Great Australian Bight.

c. Cyclone Mary will be followed by Cyclone Nina.

d. The 'Freemantle Doctor' is the cool change that arrives in Perth on a hot, summer day.

e. Summer rains often cause minor flooding on the east coast of Australia.

Spelling

Words ending In consonant 'y' change the 'y' to 'I' to add 'es'.
Add 'es' to each word.

a. factory ______________ **b.** property ______________

c. history ______________ **d.** study ______________

e. baby ______________ **f.** curry ______________

g. hurry ______________ **h.** story ______________

Syllabification: Write each word in syllables.

a. Australian ______________ **b.** patterns ______________

c. southerly ______________ **d.** properties ______________

e. alphabet ______________ **f.** seasonal ______________

Word Building

Build words using:, **ed, ing, able, ably, un,** with **'believe'**.

a. ______________

b. ______________

c. ______________

d. ______________

e. ______________

f. ______________

Punctuation

Use capital letters for **proper nouns** (people and places).

Re-write each sentence using capital letters where needed.

a. john and mary are going to port douglas for their holidays.

____

b. the australian war memorial is in canberra.

____

c. sydney, brisbane and hobart are all on the east coast of australia.

____

Decimal Fractions

1. Write the decimal fraction for the coloured part of each set of squares.

a. 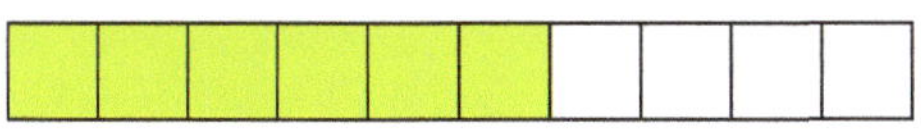 = ______

b. 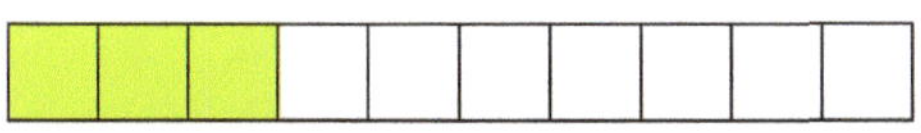 = ______

c. 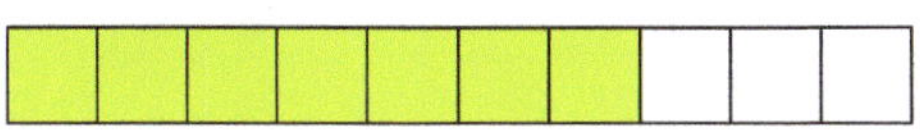 = ______

2. Write the fraction missing from each table.

	Fraction	Decimal
a.	$\frac{1}{2}$	
c.	$\frac{3}{10}$	
e.		0.7
g.	$\frac{4}{5}$	

	Fraction	Decimal
b.	$\frac{9}{10}$	
d.		0.2
f.	$\frac{1}{4}$	
h.		0.6

3. Colour the squares to show each fraction.

a. $\frac{1}{2}$ 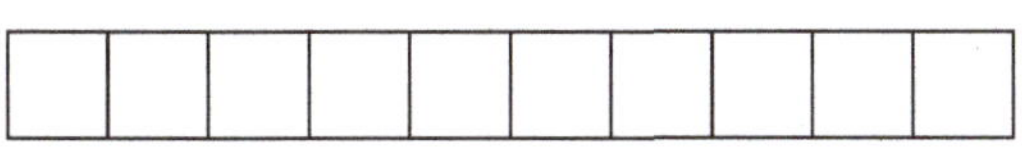

b. $\frac{6}{10}$ 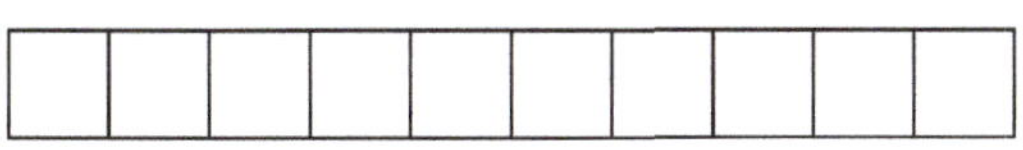

Percentages

1. Write the percentage for the shaded part on each hundredth grid.

a. 

______ %

b. 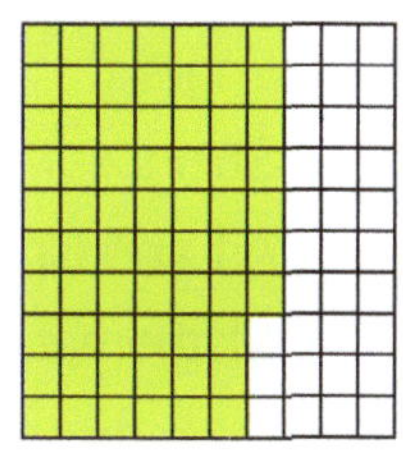

______ %

2. Change each decimal to a percentage.

a. 0.74 = ______ % **b.** 0.85 = ______ %

c. 0.32 = ______ % **d.** 0.68 = ______ %

3. Complete the table below.

	Fraction	Decimal	Percentage
a.	$\frac{3}{4}$		
b.		0.4	
c.			32%
d.	$\frac{9}{10}$		
e.		0.25	

How to make a Kite

You will need:

- Newspaper
- A ruler
- Ribbon or a plastic bag
- Craft scissors
- Duct tape
- A ball of string

Instructions:

1. Cut three diamond shaped pieces of newspaper each 30 cm by 18 cm and place them on top of each other. Secure all pieces together with duct tape.
2. Cut a piece of string 25 cm long. Tape the edges of the string to the two side points of the newspaper.
3. Allow the string to stretch across the width of the newspaper.
4. Cut a piece of string 15 cm long. Tape one edge to the top corner of the kite and the other end around the middle of the first piece of string.
5. Pull the loose end of the middle of the ball of string and tie it to the middle of the 25 cm length of string.
6. Cut the plastic bag into strips approx. 2.5 cm wide, tie them together and tape them to the bottom end of the kite to form a long tail. **Alternatively** attach a 1.5 metre long ribbon to make the tail.
7. Use the wind outside to fly your kite by holding the ball of string which should extend into the sky.

Understanding

Shade the bubble for the best answer.

a. The purpose of this text is to

- ◯ entertain
- ◯ inform
- ◯ instruct
- ◯ persuade

b. A word closer in meaning to *alternatively* is

- ◯ circulate
- ◯ otherwise
- ◯ change
- ◯ revolve

c. This activity closely relates to

- ◯ English
- ◯ Science
- ◯ Art and Craft
- ◯ Mathematics

d. Each point in the method begins with

- ◯ adjective
- ◯ adverb
- ◯ verb
- ◯ preposition

Interpreting

Circle Yes or No to answer each statement.

a. The tail of the kite can only be made from plastic strips.	**Yes**	**No**
b. Wind is needed to help the kite fly.	**Yes**	**No**
c. The lighter the frame the better the kite will fly.	**Yes**	**No**
d. The ball of string will allow the kite to fly high in the sky.	**Yes**	**No**
e. The lighter the tail the better the kite will fly.	**Yes**	**No**

Grammar

Finish each sentence with an **action verb** from the word

secure, allow, attach, extend

a. Be sure to ______________ enough string for the kite to ______________ high in the sky.

b. Don't forget to ______________ the tail to the kite and ______________ it firmly.

Spelling

Unit 5

Circle the errors in each sentence and then write each word correctly on the line.

a. He had a peice of string for the tale of his kyte.

____

b. I will nead duck tape to join the newspapa.

____

c. Their will be meny lose ends to fix up.

____

d. The ribbun will be ninty metres in lengf.

____

Word Building

Use the homophones **pour, poor, paw,** correctly in each sentence.

a. The dog burned its ____________ in the fire.

b. I was asked to ____________ the tea.

c. The ____________ girl did not have enough milk to ____________ into the cat's bowl.

Dictionary Practice: Write these words in alphabetical order.

kite, plastic, scissors, tape, piece, string, kill, ribbon, tamper, rhyme

____

Punctuation

Contractions – Abbreviated or shortened words.

it's, they're, you'll, can't, there's, wouldn't, shan't, we're

Write each **contraction** in full

a. ____________ **b.** ____________

c. ____________ **d.** ____________ **e.** ____________

f. ____________ **g.** ____________ **h.** ____________

Rounding Off

1. Round off each number to the nearest 10.

a. 78 ______ **b.** 96 ______ **c.** 54 ______

d. 82 ______ **e.** 27 ______ **f.** 41 ______

g. 53 ______ **h.** 19 ______ **i.** 88 ______

2. Round off each sum of money to the **nearest** five cents.

a. \$2.37 ______ **b.** \$4.98 ______

c. \$10.46 ______ **d.** \$7.22 ______

e. \$12.54 ______ **f.** \$8.78 ______

3. Round off each number to the **nearest** thousand.

a. 8 216 ______ **b.** 5 354 ______

c. 2 573 ______ **d.** 3 816 ______

e. 4 210 ______ **f.** 3 988 ______

Patterns

1. Find the rule for each number pattern.

a. 2 500, 500, 20, 4 Rule ______

b. 2, 4, 8, 16, 32 Rule ______

c. 14, 140, 1 400, 14 000 Rule ______

d. 3, 9, 27, 243 Rule ______

2. Add the missing number or fraction to each pattern.

a. 0.2, 0.4, ☐, 0.8, 1.0, 1.2

b. $\frac{1}{10}$, $\frac{2}{10}$, $\frac{3}{10}$, ☐, $\frac{5}{10}$, $\frac{6}{10}$

c. $\frac{1}{8}$, $\frac{1}{4}$, ☐, $\frac{1}{2}$, $\frac{5}{8}$, ☐

d. 3.3, 4.2, 5.1, ☐, 6.9, 7.8

e. $\frac{1}{6}$, $\frac{1}{3}$, $\frac{1}{2}$, $\frac{2}{3}$, ☐, 1

About this poetry: *This form of poetry is easy to write. It does not need to rhyme, is short and can be on any topic. Haiku is usually written in the present tense about nature but it can be on any chosen topic. Brainstorm ideas and words and decide on a 5 syllable, 7 syllable, 5 syllable structure for your poem.*

Here are examples for you:

Title: *Hungry Birds*

Butcher bird cries out (5)
Its whimper says I'm hungry (7)
Time to feed the flock. (5)

Title: *School Days*

Many happy days (5)
Spent in the classroom learning (7)
With friends forever. (5)

Now it's your turn.

Title: ____________________

____

____

____

Title: ____________________

____

____

____

Understanding

Shade the bubble for the best answer.

a. "Its whimper" is an example of
- ◯ metaphor
- ◯ personification
- ◯ onomatopoeia
- ◯ alliteration

b. Another word for 'flock' could be
- ◯ tuft
- ◯ lock
- ◯ wool
- ◯ number

c. An example of alliteration is
- ◯ hungry birds
- ◯ hungry butcher birds
- ◯ beautiful butcher birds
- ◯ beautiful hungry butcher birds

d. The origin of the word *Haiku* is
- ◯ Spanish
- ◯ Russian
- ◯ English
- ◯ Japanese

Interpreting

Circle **Yes** or **No** to answer each statement.

a. It is easy to write *Haiku* poetry.	**Yes**	**No**
b. Haiku poetry is long and can be on any topic.	**Yes**	**No**
c. This type of poetry doesn't need to rhyme.	**Yes**	**No**
d. There is a definite structure to follow when writing *Haiku*.	**Yes**	**No**
e. It is written in the present tense.	**Yes**	**No**

Grammar

Use an **adverb** from the word bank to complete each sentence.

beside, underneath, tomorrow, quickly, because

a. The birds came ____________ to feed ____________ it was getting late.

b. The parcel was found ____________ the letter box.

c. After the game ____________ we are going to picnic ____________ the river.

Spelling

Words ending in 'y' just add 's' to form the plural. Add 's' to these words.

a. donkey ______ b. monkey ______

c. valley ______ d. journey ______

e. trolley ______ f. turkey ______

Syllabification: Write each word in syllables.

a. Haiku ______ b. hungry ______

c. whimper ______ d. examples ______

e. forever ______ f. butcher ______

Word Building

Build **compound** words by adding **'some'** as a prefix to each word.

where, thing, one, body, day, times

a. ______

b. ______

c. ______

d. ______

e. ______

f. ______

Punctuation

Write the abbreviated form of these words. Use an apostrophe.

a. they will ______ b. he is ______ c. have not ______

d. I am ______ e. you have ______ f. can not ______

g. should have ______ h. would have ______ i. I would ______

j. it is ______

Length

1. Write each measurement in decimal notation.

a. 300 cm ______m b. 258 cm ______m

2. Use a ruler to measure the perimeter of each shape.

Perimeter = ☐ cm Perimeter = ☐ cm

3. Write the unit - centimetres (cm), millimetres (mm), or metres (m) for each item.

a. length of a pen ______

b. length of a stamp ______

c. length of the kitchen ______

d. length of your eye lashes ______

e. perimeter of this book ______

Area

1. Count the one and the half centimetre squares to find the area of each shape.

a.

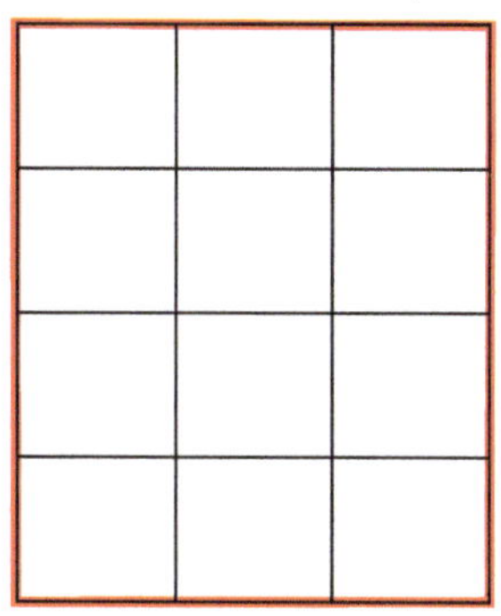

b.

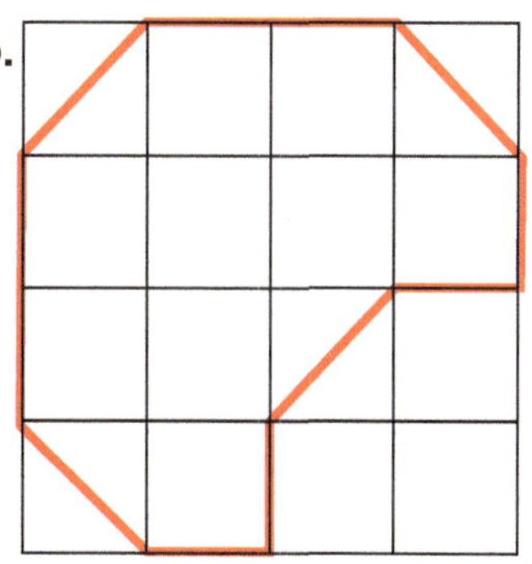

Area = ☐ cm² Area = ☐ cm²

2. Write the appropriate unit of area in cm² or m² for each object.

a.

600 ______

b.

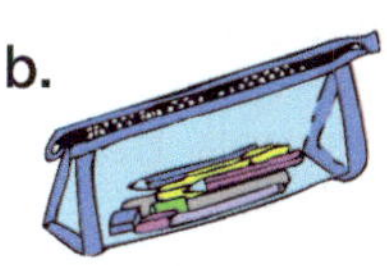

375 ______

c.

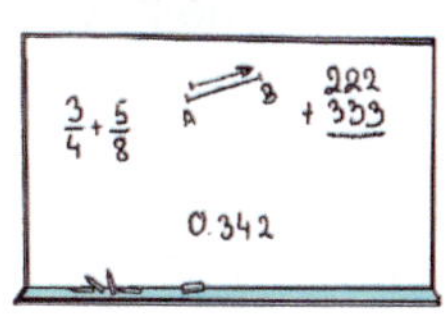

3.75 ______

d.

150 ______

Who Lives in a Rainforest?

Rainforests are tropical and therefore hot and humid and are like one enormous greenhouse. The range in temperature inside these forests is static all year round and rainfall remains constant at an average of 150cm yearly.

There are several layers which provide homes for thousands of plants, flowers and animals beneath the canopy of trees growing in these jungle hothouses. On the forest floor there is very little new growth because sunlight rarely penetrates there. This is where you might find snakes living on the herbs and seedlings that fall constantly from taller trees in the overhead layers. Where a small amount of light finds its way through, you will find small shrubs growing up to 5 metres. Millions of insects, including beautiful butterflies, will frolic in the rainforest warmth. Frogs develop in the myriad of small, water spots lying on the forest floor.

Where the layer is not so densely packed flowers and ferns grow. In this layer too, many thousands of birds can be found. Quite a large number of these birds are rare and cannot be found in any other part of the World. Many lizards, such as the Iguana, inhabit the rainforest. Large boas, which squeeze their victims to death, live in the trees and big cats such as the Jaguar, live in South American rainforests and feed on other animals of the forest including fish. As the trees become taller animals that climb and swing from tree to tree can be seen hanging upside down or even heard from miles away. Different species of bats also live in rainforests and large birds of prey hunt and kill the smaller animals such as monkeys.

Understanding

Tick the box if the information is in the text.

- **a.** The tree canopy shades the forest and creates a hothouse. ☐
- **b.** Animals, plants and trees all form different layers of the rainforest. ☐
- **c.** Small shrubs grow in the rainforest and frogs develop in water holes. ☐
- **d.** Lizards, snakes, monkeys and birds all have habitats in the rainforest. ☐
- **e.** Jaguars are large cats found in the South American rainforests. ☐
- **f.** Monkeys, bats and birds of prey traverse further up the layers of rainforest. ☐

Interpreting

Write an answer to each question.

- **a.** Name some animals you might find in a rainforest. ____________________
- **b.** What animal squeezes its victim to death? ____________________
- **c.** Name a lizard you might find in the rainforest. ____________________
- **d.** Which animals do you think swing and hang upside down in the trees? ____________________
- **e.** To what height do trees and shrubs grow in the rainforest? ____________________

Grammar

Main Clause or Dependent Clause?

Remember: A main clause is a complete idea BUT a dependent clause needs a main clause.
Underline the main clause in each sentence and write the dependent clause on the line.

- **a.** "Hurry up!," before it is dark. ____________________
- **b.** The computer didn't work after we used it. ____________________
- **c.** Now is the time if you can show me how. ____________________
- **d.** I can bake the cake when the oven is hot. ____________________
- **e.** Because the bus was late she missed the first lesson. ____________________

Spelling

When adding the suffix **'full'** to a word one 'l' is dropped.
Follow the rule and add the suffix to each word

a. care + full ____________ **b.** doubt + full ____________

c. power + full ____________ **d.** success + full ____________

e. play + full____________ **f.** peace + full ____________

Dictionary Use: Technical Words and their meaning.
Write the meaning of each word. Use your dictionary.

a. tropical ____________ **b.** penetrates ____________

c. dense ____________ **d.** species ____________

e. myriad ____________ **f.** birds of prey ____________

Word Building

Add the **suffix 'ist'** and name each occupation. Example: One who takes out teeth is a dentist.

a. one who paints pictures.

____

b. one who sells flowers

____

c. one who plays an organ

____

d. one who rides a bicycle

____

Punctuation

Commas separate phrases, clauses and adjectives when describing nouns.
Mark the commas in each sentence where needed.

a. Because of the rain the class was unhappy. **b.** When the sun came out we were happy.

c. Tom had a red green gold and yellow pencil. **d.** After dark we will look at the moon.

e. Players four five six nine and ten are here. **f.** Before the sun rises we will go fishing.

Capacity

1. How many millilitres in these?

a. 3.5 L ________ mL **b.** $\frac{1}{2}$ L ________ mL

c. 1 Litre ________ mL **d.** $2\frac{1}{4}$ L________ mL

e. 2.5 L ________ mL **f.** $5\frac{1}{4}$ L ________ mL

2. What capacity level is showing on each cylinder?

a.
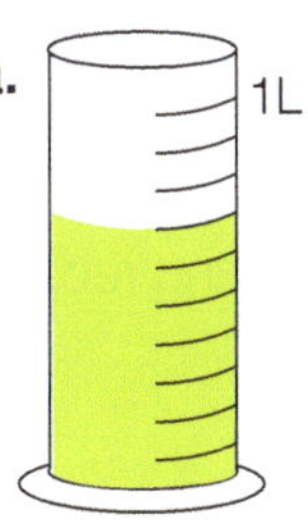

________ mL

b.
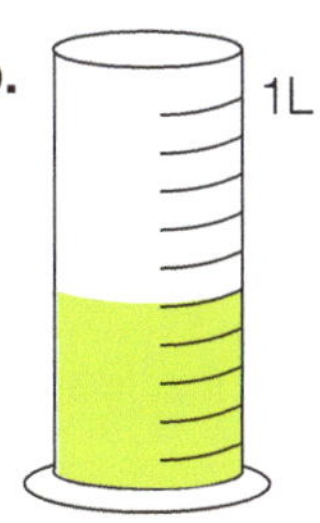

________ mL

c.
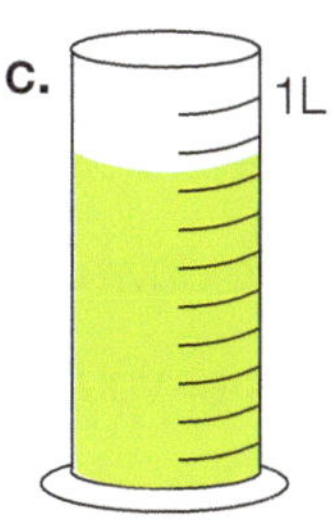

________ mL

3. Write the millilitres in decimal form.

a. 375 mL ________ **b.** 600 mL ________

c. 400 mL ________ **d.** 750 mL ________

e. 250mL ________ **f.** 1 350 mL ________

Volume

1. Count the centicubes in each shape.

a.
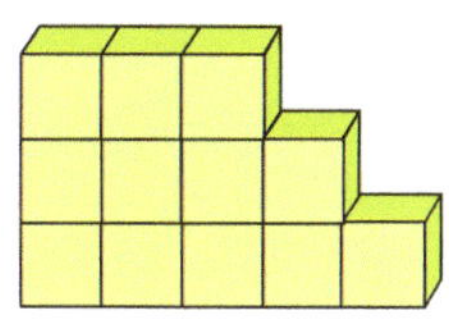
[ ] centicubes

b.

[ ] centicubes

2. Find the volume of each shape by multiplying L x W x H = volume³.

a.
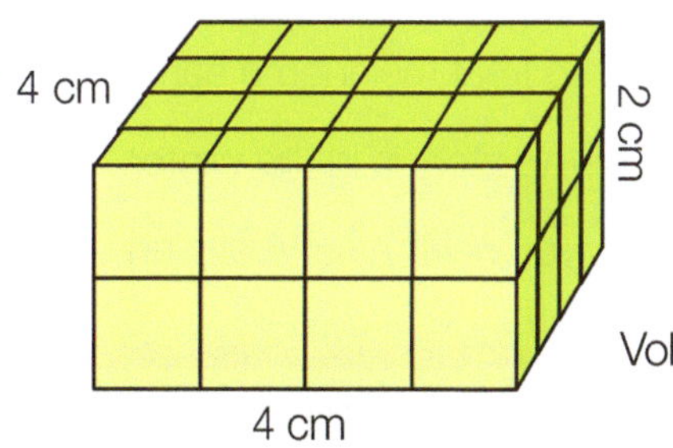

Volume [ ] cm³

b.
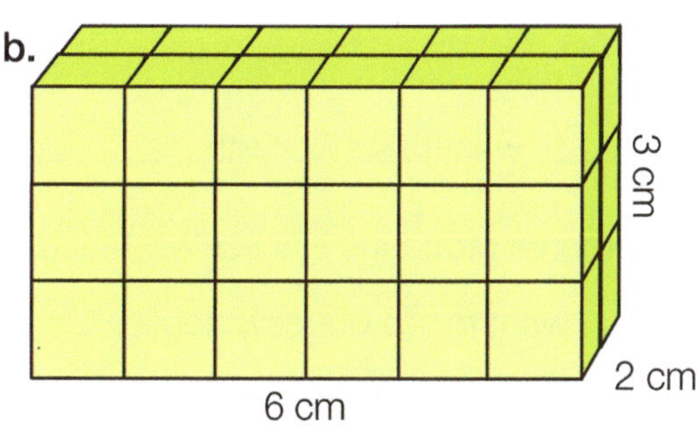

Volume [ ] cm³

Cover-Up to Prevent Skin Damage

Slip, Slop, Slap!

A very important message for anyone who intends going outdoors to work or play under the burning rays of our sun. If you intend being outside during the day do not be fooled into thinking that because the sun is overcast it will not burn you. Whether it is a bright sunny day or just a dull day, it is just as important to follow the messages given by your parents and teachers about covering up your skin to protect it from being burnt. On both days the sun can and will, burn you.

I believe we must take extra care in Australia because the sun is so harsh and there is a longer time during the hot summer days and months for it to do us harm. Skin cancer can result from over exposure to our cruel sun and it can be deadly. It takes a long time for melanoma to become evident and often, when it does, it is too late to treat. Therefore, the best cure for skin cancer is to prevent it from happening altogether. This might be easier said than done but we should try and prepare ourselves carefully when going outdoors to play, swim, walk or ride. There is no doubt that prevention is better than cure. The sun can be very dangerous so we need to prepare and cover our skin when going outside during the most dangerous times of day.

Take my advice and be sun wise when outdoor activities are the order of the day. Do you enjoy the sunshine? Then remember, cover up and protect your skin. Always - Slip, Slop, Slap!

Understanding

Shade the bubble for the best answer.

a. What is melanoma?
- ◯ peeling of the skin
- ◯ damage to the skin
- ◯ growth or skin tumour
- ◯ disease eating bug

b. What does it mean by 'slip, slop, slap'?
- ◯ take care doing outdoor activities
- ◯ use a cover to protect the skin
- ◯ give the skin a hard workout
- ◯ fall over, spill it then hit it hard

c. What is the main purpose of this text?
- ◯ to inform
- ◯ to instruct
- ◯ to persuade
- ◯ to prevent

d. What is the cause of melanoma?
- ◯ exposure of the skin
- ◯ exposure to the daylight
- ◯ over exposure to the sun
- ◯ exposure to the sunlight

Interpreting

Tick the box if the information is in the text.

a. The sun will burn on dull days. ☐
b. Always wear a hat in the hot sun. ☐
c. The Australian sun burns skin more. ☐
d. Skin cancer kills people. ☐
e. It is important to treat melanoma early. ☐
f. Prevention is better than cure. ☐
g. The setting of this story is in the winter. ☐
h. The dawn sky was a glowing and shimmering red. ☐
i. In case of fire, you need a survival plan. ☐
j. Either you stay and fight a fire or evacuate. ☐

Grammar

Use personal pronouns correctly in the sentences below: **I, me, him, you, their, yours, ours**

a. That book is ____________________ .
b. Will ______________ give that to ______________.
c. ____________ went to school with ____________ .
d. ______________ car is similar to ______________.

Underline the **personal pronouns** in these sentences.

a. Mum and I went to see our new house.
b. We went with dad and my sister too.
c. Are you able to come to his concert?
d. It was still alive when they found their lost kitten.

Spelling

Some nouns have a different spelling in the plural. Write the plural of each word.

a. man ____________ **b.** tooth ____________

c. foot ____________ **d.** woman ____________

e. mouse ____________ **f.** goose ____________

g. louse ____________ **h.** child ____________

Dictionary Use: Technical Words and their Meanings.
Write the meaning of each word. A dictionary could help.

a. rays ____________ **b.** overcast ____________

c. exposure ____________ **d.** melanoma ____________

Write the words in alphabetical order. ____________

____

Word Building

Build nouns using suffix **OR**

a. One who helps the sick

____

b. One who makes suits

____

c. One who writes books

____

d. One who carves figures in stone

____

e. One who plots the course of a ship or plane

____

Punctuation

Use the **persuasive language** in the Word Bank to fill in the blanks.

Take my advice, I think, we should do it, without a doubt

a. ____________, prevent cancer by protecting the skin from the sun.

b. When going swimming, ____________ it is wise to Slip, Slop, Slap!

c. It is easy to prevent melanoma and ____________.

Angles

1. Classify each angle as acute, obtuse, right, reflex or straight angle.

a. 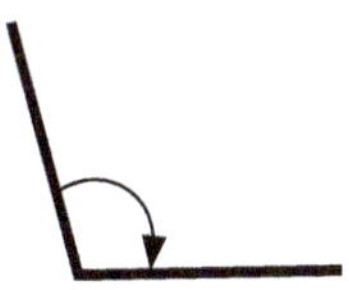 ________

b. 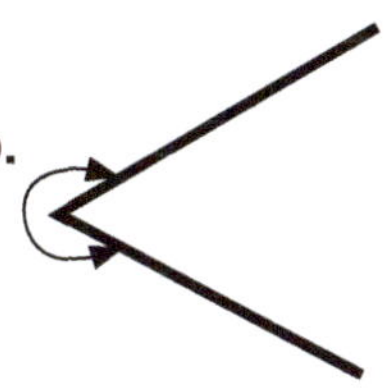 ________

c. 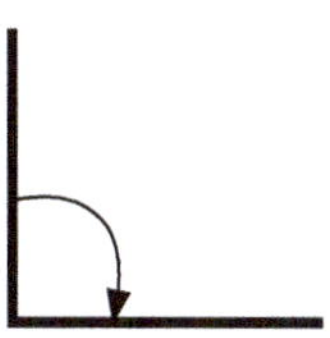 ________

d. 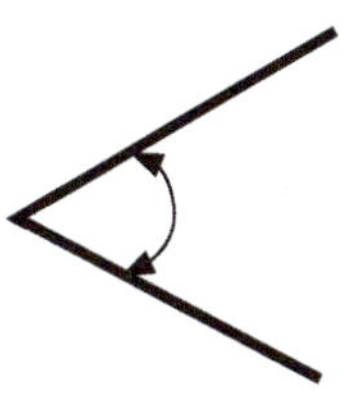 ________

2. Complete each sentence about types of angles.

a. An angle between 0 degrees and 90 degrees is called a ____________ angle.

b. An angle of 180 degrees is a ____________ angle.

c. An angle between 90 degrees and 180 degrees is an ____________angle.

2D Shapes

1. Name each 2D shape.

a. ________

b. ________

c.  ________

d. 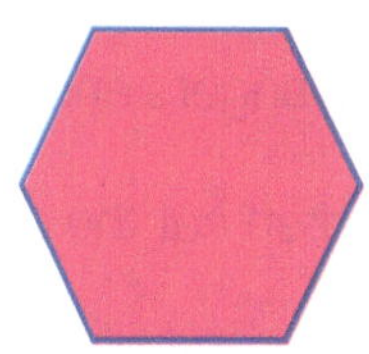 ________

e.  ________

2. Draw, then count the diagonals in each shape.

a.  Diagonals ☐

b. 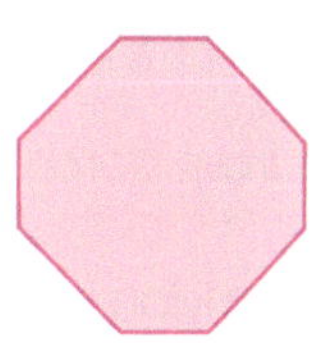 Diagonals ☐

Entrées, Mains and Desserts - Choices

Annabelle's Fabulous Children's Menu

entrée:	Fresh Prawn Cocktail with Seafood Sauce	$10.00
	Chicken Wings (3 pieces)	$6.00
	Special Fried Rice	$3.50
mains:	Chicken Nuggets, Chips and Gravy	$7.00
	Fish Fingers and Chips	$6.00
	Spaghetti with Meat Sauce	$4.00
dessert:	Banana Split with Ice Cream and Flavouring	$5.00
	Fresh Fruit Salad	$4.50
	Ice Cream and flavouring	$2.50

Children Under 2 - Free Adult meals available starting at $15.00 for Bangers and Mash.

Special Mid-Week Deals – *Children 3 – 6 Half Price* – Monday and Tuesday

Understanding

Circle **Yes** or **No** for your answer.

a. Does Annabelle's menu have a good range of food? **Yes** **No**

b. Would you like to eat at Annabelle's? **Yes** **No**

c. Could you afford to eat at this restaurant? **Yes** **No**

d. Face painting is for boys and girls. **Yes** **No**

e. Would $10 buy you three courses at Annabelle's? **Yes** **No**

Interpreting

Write an answer to each question.

a. How many fish dishes are on the menu?____________________

b. What are 'Bangers and Mash'? ____________________

c. Young children eat the cheapest on which days?____________________

d. Why would it be free for children under 2? ____________________

e. How much for a Prawn Cocktail, Chicken Nuggets and a Banana Split? ____________________

Grammar

Pronouns that **relate** to people and things - who, whom, whose, which or that

Cross out the incorrect relative pronoun in each sentence

a. Who / Whose team won the Grand Final?

b. Which / That train will take you to Central?

c. To whom / Who did you give the new book?

d. Who / Whom was meant to be the head prefect?

e. Whose /That shoes are on the front porch?

f. The boys which / who are 12 can all play soccer.

g. That / Which plane is going to London.

h. Which / Whose work will be on display today?

Spelling

Root or Base Words from the Latin **Primo** meaning **First**.

primary, prime, primer, primitive

Complete each sentence with the correct word.

a. The ______________ Minister is head of the Government.

b. He began school at Central ______________ School.

c. The painter told us we needed to begin with a ______________ for a good result.

d. A ____________ number has only one and itself as a factor.

e. The early settlers in Australia made ______________ bark huts for shelter.

Syllabification: Write each word in syllables.

a. fabulous ________________ **b.** entrées ________________

c. spaghetti ________________ **d.** banana ________________

e. flavouring ________________ **f.** dessert ________________

Word Building

Use the word '**improve**' and add the suffixes in the box to make new words.

s, ed, ing, ment

a. ______________________

b. ______________________

c. ______________________

d. ______________________

Now make new words using the same suffixes and the word '**invest**'.

a. ______________________

b. ______________________

c. ______________________

d. ______________________

Punctuation

Inverted Commas (Speech marks) used to show exact words spoken.

Example: Ben said, "I am going to Annabelle's for dinner. Will you come with me?"

Re-write the following sentence using correct punctuation. Do not stand on the grass cried Jack

____

Nets

Name the 3D object made by each net.

1.

____

2.

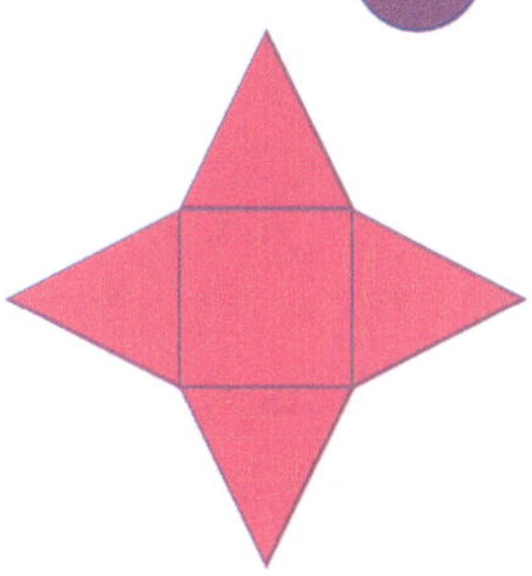

____

____

3.

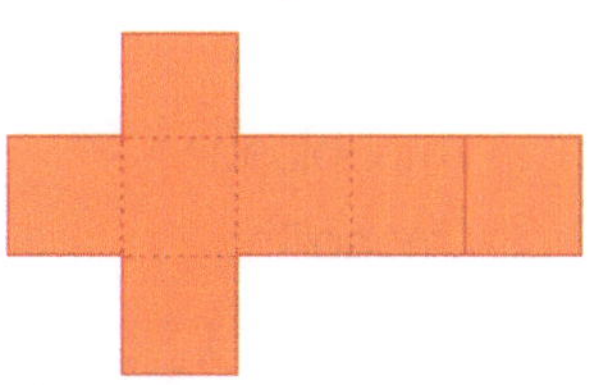

____

4.

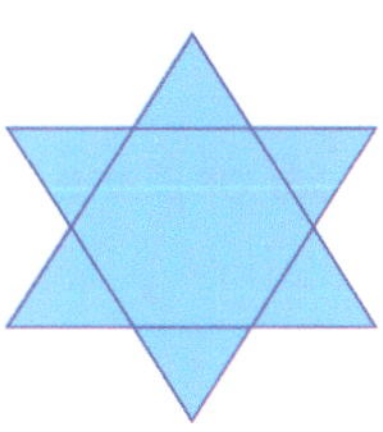

____

____

Mass

1. Write the mass showing on each bathroom scale.

a.

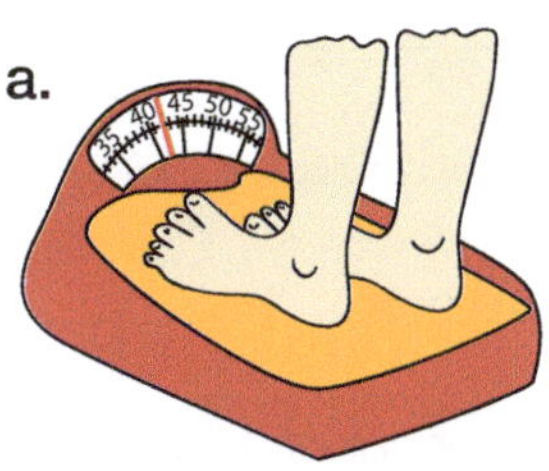

________ kg

b.

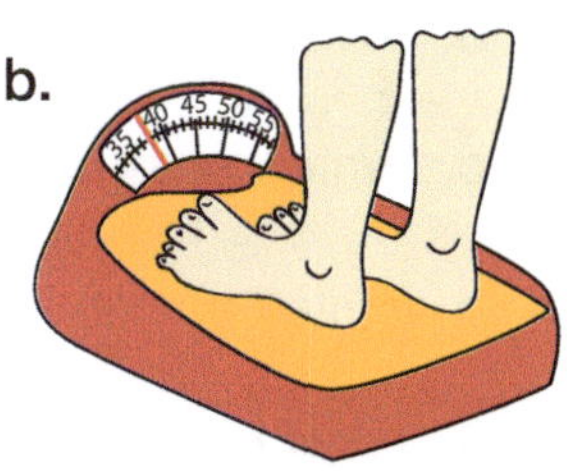

________ kg

c.

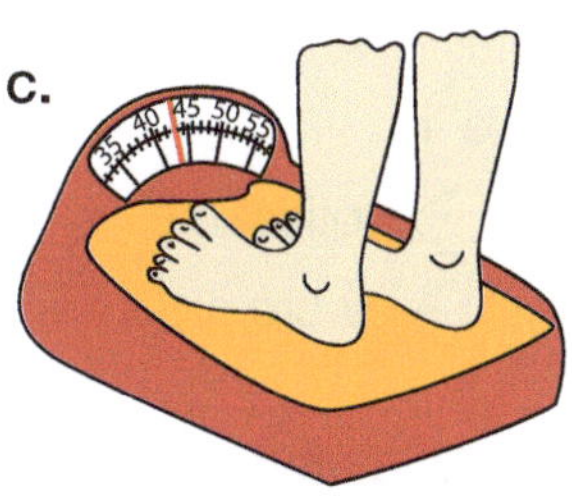

________ kg

d.

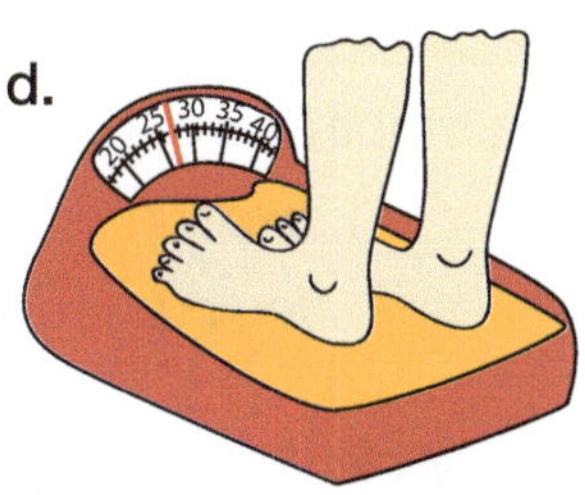

________ kg

2. Write these grams in decimal notation.

a. 835 g ____________ **b.** 1 250 g ____________

c. 165 g ____________ **d.** 2 000 g ____________

e. 1 500 g ____________ **f.** 2 235 g ____________

Our Visit to Uluru

Our excitement was palpable! We had been looking forward to seeing the 'rock' since we arrived at the campsite two days back. It was all that we talked about. Just imagine! This huge monolith, the largest in the World, is in our own backyard. Wow!

Many exciting aspects of geological phenomenon were visible and it is those that draw visitors to the Territory regularly to experience and observe such natural wonders. Morning sunrise delighted us! We found the seemingly changing appearance of the monolith unbelievable, while afternoon sunsets were just as spectacular. Visible changes occurred to the colour and shape of 'the rock' during those times of the day. At one time the appearance resembled a bright orange hue through to the deepest of reds and many different hues of the spectrum became evident. We realised, of course, that it all depended upon the weather and time of the year. During late afternoon in winter, when the heavy night fog descends upon it you might be lucky to experience Uluru resembling a Christmas pudding complete with soft flowing cream over its sides,.

We saw waterfalls and crevices, caves and sacred spots on Uluru. Inside the caves we saw paintings from years gone by, telling stories of the tribal Aborigines who once lived there. In the mid-1980s, the area was returned to the Anangu peoples, who have inhabited the area for some 22,000 years. Now it is listed in the Uluru-Kata Tjuta National Park, a part of the Macdonnell Ranges, in the Northern Territory.*

Our dad told us that when he was a boy he visited Ayres Rock. It was called that before it reverted to its native nomenclature. Then it was possible to walk on it, but many tourists did not obey the safety signs, which clearly instructed walkers to hold onto the chain and stay on the marked track. This led to some falling off, some dying and some having to be rescued after falling into its crevices.

What a spectacular sight! It's no wonder crowds keep visiting this sacred site to enjoy its beauty.

Understanding

Write an answer to each question.

a. Why can't visitors climb the 'rock'? ____________________

b. Where is Uluru? ____________________

c. Write words meaning remarkable Earth's changes? ____________________

d. Write two names for this 'rock'. ____________________

e. What causes changes to occur on Uluru? ____________________

Interpreting

Shade the bubble for the correct answer.

a. Another word for 'palpable' is
- ◯ exciting
- ◯ noticeable
- ◯ feeling
- ◯ aware

b. The word 'spectrum' means
- ◯ range
- ◯ objects
- ◯ colours
- ◯ detail

c. Which best explains nomenclature?
- ◯ likeness
- ◯ difference
- ◯ site
- ◯ name

d. A single huge rock is a
- ◯ monopoly
- ◯ monologue
- ◯ monocle
- ◯ monolith

Grammar

Underline the **adverbial phrase** in each sentence.

a. Many events happen during late afternoon.

b. Visitors arrive at Uluru by bus, car or plane.

c. At one time of day changes occur.

d. The fog rolls in over its sides.

e. In the mid-1980s, the name changed.

f. Inside the caves we saw paintings.

Unit 10

Spelling

Drop one 'l' when 'all' is used as a prefix. Re-write each word correctly. Follow the rule.

a. all most ____________ b. all ways ____________

c. all though ____________ d. all ready ____________

e. all so ____________ f. all together ____________

Exception to this rule: **All right** is written as two words always.

Alphabetical Order: Write the difficult words in AO.

palpable, geology, crevices, monolith, spectrum, nomenclature

____

Word Building

Build **compound words** by re-writing the word and adding **'where'** to it.

a. some ____________

b. no ____________

c. any ____________

d. where ____________

Punctuation

Proper Nouns begin with a **capital letter**.

Complete each sentence using the correct proper noun.

Uluru   Ayres Rock   The Olgas   Northern Territory   Kata-Tjuta

a. Before the 1980s ____________ was known as ____________ ____________.

b. All of these great sites are in the ____________ ____________.

c. ________ ____________ are now known as ____________ ____________.

24 Hour Time

1. Write the clock face afternoon time in 24 hour notation.

a. 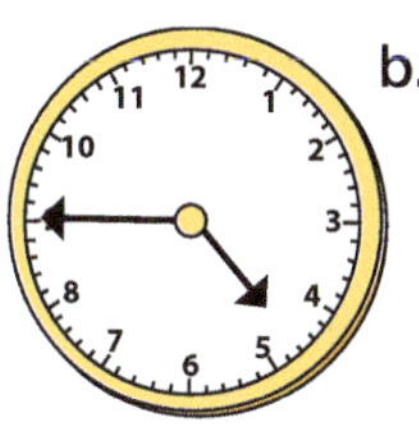

b. 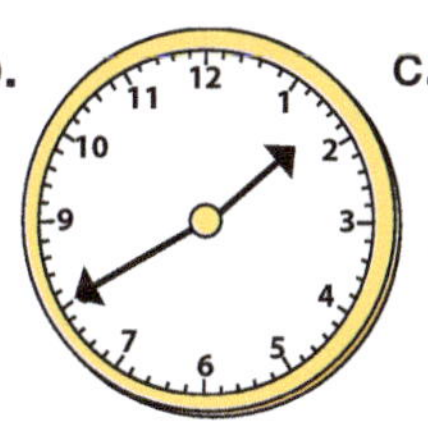

c. 

[:]   [:]   [:]

2. Write each time in 24 hours notation.

a. 6 : 30 pm   [:]

b. 8 : 45 am   [:]

3. Show each time on the clock face.

a. 14:25

b. 19:35

c. 16:40

Temperature

1. Show the temperatures on the Celsius scale thermometers.

a. 25°C   b. 40°C   c. 65°C   d. 15°C

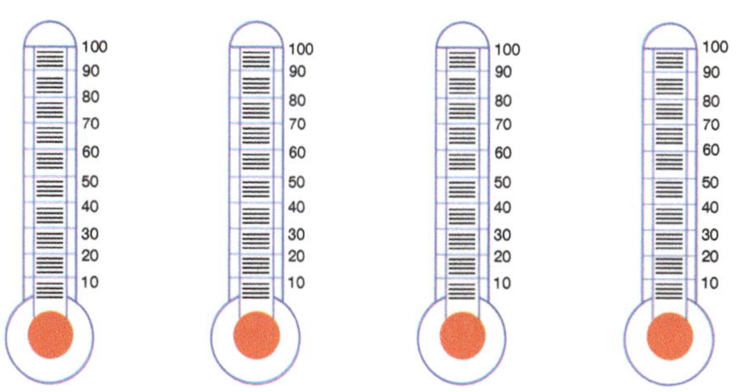

2. Write each temperature in short form. Eg. 25°C

a. boiling point of water. ________

b. forty-two degrees Celsius. ________

3. Write the temperature showing on each thermometer.

a. 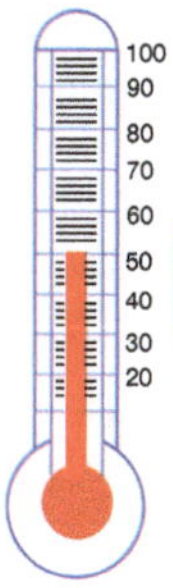 [ ]°

b. 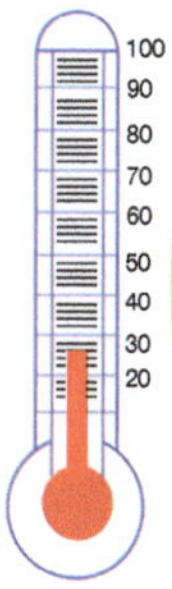 [ ]°

c. 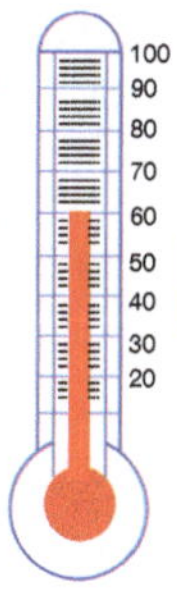 [ ]°

The Koala

One of Australia's native animals is the well-known and much loved Koala. Fossils dating back over 20 million years have been found of this animal. Koalas eat eucalyptus leaves of a particular type and almost nothing else. Because of this particular aspect of their diet they are found only where the particular eucalypt grows. Koalas have a soft fur, sharp claws to help them climb trees and large noses coloured pink or black. They also have fingerprints similar to humans. Their brains have become smaller over time which is thought to be a result of the low energy they ingest from their diets. Their closest living relative is believed to be the wombat.

When a koala is born it lives in its mother's pouch for up to six months where it grows and then it stays with its mother for another six months or so afterwards. One particular feature of the Koala is they sleep for anything from 18 up to 23 hours each day. Outside of the breeding season a koala makes very little noise.

It does not like to be patted at the back of its head but it is happy to be nursed and have its back rubbed. While Koalas are delightful animals, attracting the attention of both young and old, they cannot be kept as pets. And the baby Koala is called a 'joey'.

Colonies of Koalas are in danger of becoming extinct caused by logging in rural areas and urbanisation which is destroying their feeding opportunities. Road accidents and disease, together with attacks from wild dogs, are other factors causing the demise of koala populations in Australia. In an attempt to prevent the extinction of this popular Australian marsupial, animal lovers and specialist wildlife enthusiasts provide support to the animals that are mauled and to those with various injuries sustained either in the bush or on the road. Through the dedicated care and attention of these wildlife warriors, injured 'joeys' are nursed back to good health and given a second chance of survival. When they are fully recovered from their injuries and are given a clean bill of health, they are released back into the bush where their chances of survival might best be achieved.

Understanding

Tick the box if the information is in the text.

- **a.** Koalas are found only in Australia. ☐
- **b.** Koalas are related to the Wombat. ☐
- **c.** Fossils date Koalas back more than 20 million years. ☐
- **d.** Koalas have large brains. ☐
- **e.** Koalas do not have human-like features. ☐
- **f.** The koala likes to be patted on its head. ☐
- **g.** Road kill contributes to loss of Koala Colonies. ☐
- **h.** A baby koala is called a 'joey'. ☐

Interpreting

Match a word to its meaning.

ingest, demise, extinct, enthusiastic, eucalypt, dedicated

- **a.** to die or decrease ______________
- **b.** to be keen, interested ______________
- **c.** a particular gum tree ______________
- **d.** to take in, to eat ______________
- **e.** to give time and effort ______________
- **f.** no longer around ______________

Grammar

Comparative and Superlative Adjectives – big, bigger, biggest; good, better, best; bad, worse, worst

Complete each sentence using the correct form of the adjective.

- **a.** This is a ______________ book but this one is ______________ and this one is the ______________.
- **b.** The apple was ______________ but that one was ______________ and this one is the ______________.
- **c.** John is ______________ and Tom is ______________ but Kamal is the ______________.

Spelling

Circle the errors in each sentence and then write each word correctly on the line.

a. Won of Australia's best loved aminals is the Koala.

____

b. Kowalas have soft fir, sharp clause and larje noses.

____

c. Loging is distroiing there feeding habbitats.

____

d. Wildlife entusiasts are also called wildlife worriers.

____

Word Building

Compound Words Write each word as two words.

a. sometime ____________________

b. anywhere ____________________

c. bedroom ____________________

d. fingerprints ____________________

e. sunrise ____________________

f. homework ____________________

Missing Letters: Fill in the missing vowels in each word.

a. ___ ___ c ___ l ___ p t s

b. c ___ l ___ ___ r ___ d

c. ___ f t ___ r w ___ r d s

d. d ___ l ___ g h t f ___ l

e. ___ p p ___ r t ___ n ___ t ___ ___ s

f. ___ t t r ___ c t ___ n g

Punctuation

Apostrophes of Possession Example: Tom's cat James' car

Insert an apostrophe correctly in each of these.

a. Tom Thumbs boat

b. Smiths House

c. childrens games

d. various species habitats

e. the ladys coat

f. the Joneses car

Graphs

Here is a graph showing the number of dresses made in a clothing factory in one week. Use it to answer the questions below.

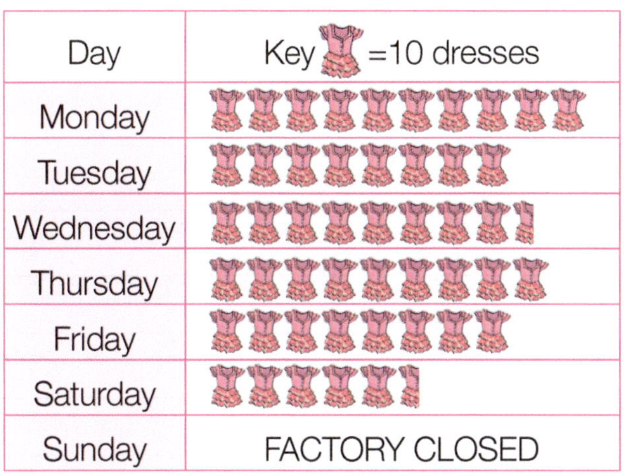

1. How many dresses were made on Tuesday? ________

2. On which day were the most dresses made?

____

3. How many more dresses were made on Wednesday than on Tuesday? ________

4. On which day were 100 dresses produced?

____

Location

1. Write the co-ordinates for each shape marked on the grid.

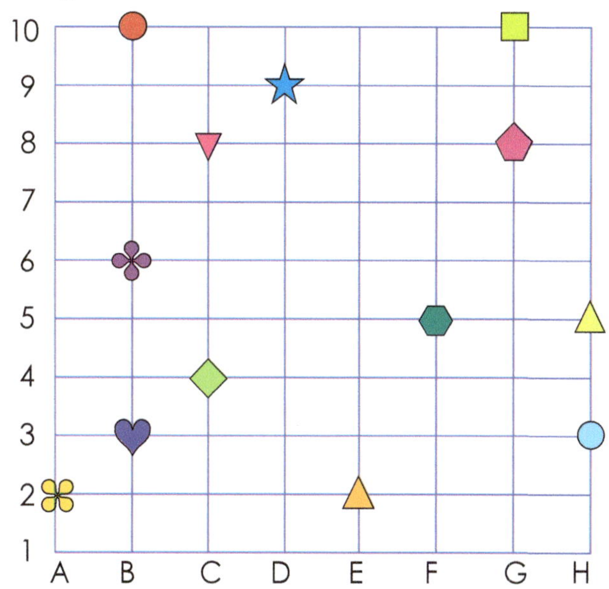

1.  ____________

2.  ____________

3.  ____________

4.  ____________

5.  ____________

6.  ____________

7.  ____________

8.  ____________

9.  ____________

10.  ____________

Should Children Work for Pocket Money?

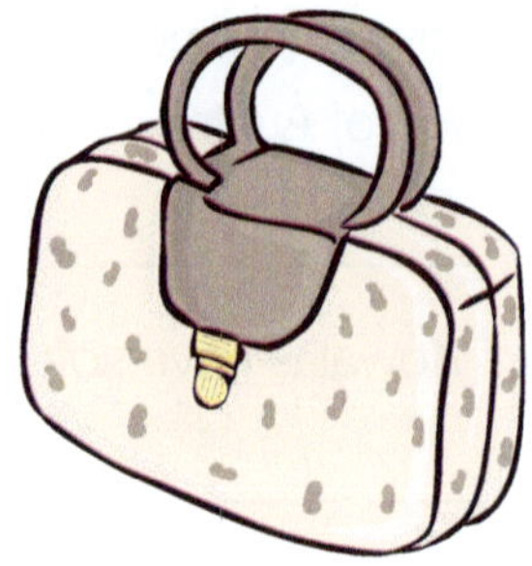

This is a very contentious issue. Many parents will have a very different opinion from their children about this question and no doubt each opinion can stand up to scrutiny. But let us explore when pocket money should be given to children and then decide if pocket money is to be gratuitous or a reward for performance or behaviour.

In my opinion, it is possible for very young children to receive pocket money, but to learn the value of money and to realise it's something to be earned. They should negotiate a task to be done and decide upon the payment for completion of that task. It could be as simple as packing away toys after they are used and that will be a benefit to everyone in the house.

When a child is older, say 8 to 10, then the task can be reviewed and another amount agreed upon while keeping in mind he or she has to earn what is given. This will instil in the children how important it is to work for a reward that can benefit themselves and others.

After reaching the teen years a price for pocket money can then be re-negotiated to reflect the age and abilities, the needs and wants of each child. Always keep in mind the one important thing about receiving money: everyone in the house must earn the money they receive whether it is used for spending or saving.

If, on the other hand, pocket money is given gratuitously then the child will not need to negotiate how to earn it or whether to save it or spend it.

Understanding

Circle **Yes** or **No** for your answer.

a. Children should work for pocket money?	**Yes**	**No**
b. Pocket money should be earned?	**Yes**	**No**
c. Parents often have the same point of view as their children.	**Yes**	**No**
d. Tasks do not need to be part of earning pocket money?	**Yes**	**No**
e. The child should be able to choose how to use any pocket money.	**Yes**	**No**

Interpreting

Write an answer to each question

a. What is the contentious issue in this text? ______________________________

b. What are the main opinions expressed by the writer? ______________________________

c. How can 9 year olds set the amount of their pocket money? ______________________________

____

d. What is important for a teenager to remember when earning pocket money? ______________________________

____

e. Circle the word closest in meaning to **'negotiate'** - seek discuss find need

Grammar

Prepositions beginning Adverbial Phrases

Examples: near the front gate between the fence under the tree across the road

Use one example in each sentence correctly.

a. We decided to take a break so we sat down ______________________________

b. All the students were taken ______________________________ to catch the bus.

c. The new garden was made ______________________________.

d. The tree that fell in the wind was the one ______________________________ and the road.

Spelling — Unit 12

Root or Base Words from the Latin **Pedis** meaning **foot**.

pedestrian, pedal, biped, pedicure, centiped

Match each word to its meaning:

a. one hundred feet ______

b. two feet ______

c. foot treatment ______

d. to go by foot ______

e. moving a lever by foot ______

Syllabification: Write each word in syllables

a. contentious ______ **b.** gratuitous ______ **c.** performance ______

d. negotiated ______ **e.** reviewed ______ **f.** individual ______

Word Building

Using the prefix **'mis'**

Make a new word using the prefix 'mis'.

a. fortune ______

b. understood ______

c. print ______

d. adventure ______

Punctuation

Contractions using ARE

Their There or They're You Your or You're

Use the words correctly in each sentence.

a. T______ going to buy t______ mother a birthday present today.

b. ______ is the place where ______ new house will be built.

c. Over ______ is where ______ going to be with ______ parents.

d. Will y______ friends take ______ and ______ sister to town?

e. Y______ going to be late for school if ______ don't hurry.

Problems

1. Ninety-nine marbles are to be shared evenly between three children. How many marbles will each one receive?

☐ ÷ ☐ = ☐ each

2. Eighty-three cakes were to be placed on eight plates.

How many cakes were left over? ☐

3. There are 96 shoes on a shelf, how many pairs are there? ☐

4. A truck travelled 652 kilometres on its first trip, 588 on its second and 1 265 on its third trip. How many kilometres did it travel on the three trips?

☐ kilometres

Probabilities

1. On a scale of 0 to 1 rate the chance of each event happening. Use this scale.

0 — 0.1 — 0.2 — 0.3 — 0.4 — 0.5 — 0.6 — 0.7 — 0.8 — 0.9 — 1

Never happen (0) 50-50 chance (0.5) certain to happen (1)

a. Mum will win lotto tonight. ______

b. My birthday is in May. ______

c. A tail will turn up on a coin toss. ______

d. It will rain tomorrow. ______

e. Birds fly north in winter. ______

2. Rate the chance or probability of the spinner landing on each colour.

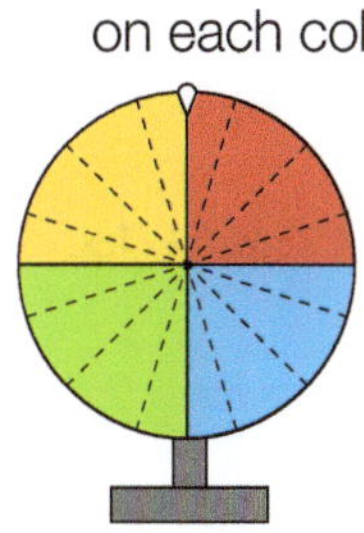

a. yellow 0.25 **b.** blue ______

c. green ______ **d.** red ______

Which Bus Stop Will You Use?

Use the table below to find the stop you should use to catch your bus. Always signal the driver to stop.

FROM	Central	Town Hall	Queen's Square	Railway Parade
TO	Board at Bus Stop Marked			
Lakeside	A	C	B	D
West End	D	B	A	C
East Gardens	B	D	C	A
Northlakes	C	A	D	B
Airport	B	D	C	A
Hospital	A	C	B	D
Inner West	D	B	A	C
Northern Beaches	C	A	D	B

Understanding

Write the bus stop to board.

a. From Queen's Square to West End ________

b. From Central to Inner West ________

c. From Central to Hospital ________

d. From Town Hall to East Gardens ________

e. From Railway Parade to Northlakes ________

f. From Central to Airport ________

g. From Town Hall to Northern Beaches ________

h. From Queen's Square to Lakeside ________

Interpreting

Use the table to answer each question.

a. How many different bus stops are there on the table? ____________________

b. What should you do when the bus is coming? ____________________

c. What will happen if you are at the wrong bus stop? ____________________

d. Where do you think the buses are going? ____________________

e. Why are only four pick-up places on the table? ____________________

Grammar

Prepositions (before the noun) or **Adverbs** (after the verb)?

Use a preposition or an adverb to complete each sentence correctly

Prepositions: with, between, towards, around **Adverbs:** outside, alone, quietly, indoors

a. ____________ their cousins and themselves they went ____________ to play.

b. They moved ____________ the house ____________ because dad was asleep.

c. ____________ no money, the girls decided it was best to stay ____________.

d. The children were home ____________ because their parents were at work.

e. ____________ the two of them there was no reason to catch the train home.

Spelling

Homographs – Same Spelling but different meaning and different pronunciation. Find the meaning of each word in your dictionary and write it on the line.

Minute ______________________

Minute ______________________

Sow ______________________

Sow ______________________

Proof Reading: Words that need correction.
Write the underlined words correctly on the line.

a. He needed to bored the bus at the korect bus stop.

____

b. You mst always signl the driver to stop the bus.

____

c. Sentrel Raylway is the main stopping point for trains.

____

d. Est Gardns is close to the Arport stop.

____

Word Building

Antonyms - Word Opposites formed by adding a Prefix. Write the opposite of each word by adding either **un** or **im**

a. happy ____________

b. likely ____________

c. suitable ____________

d. opened ____________

e. pure ____________

f. patient ____________

g. moveable ____________

h. polite ____________

Punctuation

Contractions for Shortened Words. Write the contracted form of the word in italics on the line.

a. *They are* going to the local markets. ____________

b. *We have* been off school sick. ____________

c. Did you say *you are* going home? ____________

d. *It is* not a very nice cake. ____________

e. *They were* not able to get tickets. ____________

f. *We will* be there forever. ____________

Transformation

1. Re-draw the cartoon character using the grid.

2. If you decrease a shape by 50% what will be its area? Circle your choice.

$\frac{1}{2}$ $\frac{1}{4}$ $\frac{3}{4}$

Shopping

1. How much will you spend to buy all of these items?

$ ____

2. How much will you pay for 4 books if one book costs $15? $ ____

3. Abby saves $8 each week. How much will she have in ten weeks? $ ____

4. How many $5 in $170? $ ____

5. How many 50 cents in $120? $ ____

Reading

Unit 14

Explanation

Ocean Waves and Currents

Water is constantly moving and is very strong. That is why we are told not to walk or drive through flood waters. What about water in the ocean? Well, that is no different. On the surface the water moves in the form of waves but under those waves there are strong water currents which might be undertows or rips.

Ocean currents can be very strong in places and can be seen on top of the water as in rips or felt under the water as an undertow. The wind causes currents and also the rotation of the Earth is responsible for current formations. Currents flow in an anti-clockwise direction in the southern hemisphere. The gravitational pull of the Moon and the Sun also impacts how ocean currents operate. Hence we have tides.

Ocean waves happen when the wind blows across the top of the water and friction creates energy for the water to form into waves of different sizes and strength. Waves that are formed by an underwater eruption and create a tsunami can be so powerful and full of energy they move great distances, gathering more speed and force in their travels until they hit land, with known, devastating effects.

Ocean swells are formed by distant storms and travel across the waves rolling long distances across the ocean. The difference between ocean waves and ocean swells is waves are formed by wind and are choppy while swells are rolling and smooth. A swell is measured from its top or crest, to the bottom or trough.

Understanding

Shade the bubble for the best answer.

a. Where are strong water currents found?

- ◯ In flood waters
- ◯ In the ocean pools
- ◯ Under the waves
- ◯ On top of the water

b. What causes the water currents?

- ◯ rips
- ◯ floods
- ◯ the waves
- ◯ the Earth moving

c. What creates ocean swells?

- ◯ A tsunami
- ◯ An undertow
- ◯ Distant storms
- ◯ Rolling, Smooth Water

d. How are waves formed?

- ◯ by the wind
- ◯ from rolling water
- ◯ by choppy seas
- ◯ by the pull of the Moon

Interpreting

Write an answer to each question.

a. How would currents flow in the Northern Hemisphere? ____________________

b. What is the difference between the Ocean and flood water? ____________________

c. What causes the ocean currents to function? ____________________

d. What causes a tsunami? ____________________

e. What are other names for strong ocean currents? ____________________

Grammar

Noun Groups and Technical Language.

Underline the noun groups in each sentence.

a. The water in the ocean can have dangerous rips.

b. There are waves of different sizes and strength.

c. Waves are powerful and full of energy.

d. Waves move great distances until they hit land.

e. Swells travel across the waves and ocean.

f. Measure swells from top of crests to its bottom.

Spelling

Unit 14

Homophones – Words with same sound, different spelling and different meaning. Find the meaning of each word and write it on the line.

a. board ____________ **b.** bored ____________

c. licence ____________ **d.** license ____________

e. stationery ____________ **f.** stationary ____________

g. dependant ____________ **h.** dependent ____________

i. practice ____________ **j.** practise ____________

Syllabification: Write each word in syllables.

a. rotation ____________ **b.** gravitational ____________

c. friction ____________ **d.** devastating ____________

e. hemisphere ____________ **f.** difference ____________

Word Building

Nouns ending in x, s, z, sh & ch add 'es' to form plural. Write each word in the plural.

a. box ____________

b. bus ____________

c. buzz ____________

d. languish ____________

e. catfish ____________

f. fetish ____________

g. church ____________

h. lurch ____________

i. detach ____________

Punctuation

Acronyms of Time Write each acronym in full.

a. am ____________ **b.** pm ____________

c. EST ____________ **d.** GMT ____________

e. AEDT ____________

Tessellation

1. Colour the shapes that can make a tessellating pattern.

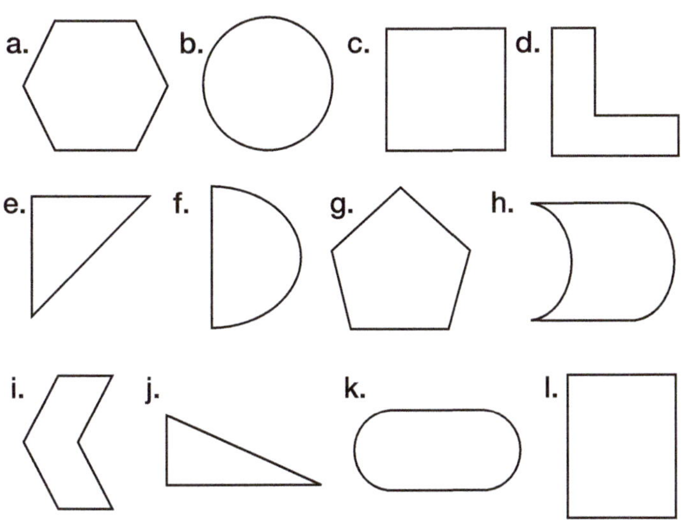

2. Draw a line to where each shape belongs to make a tile that will tessellate.

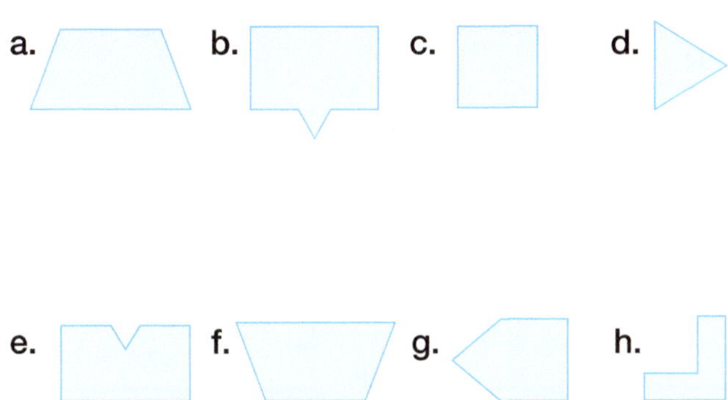

Addition

1. Name each polygon.

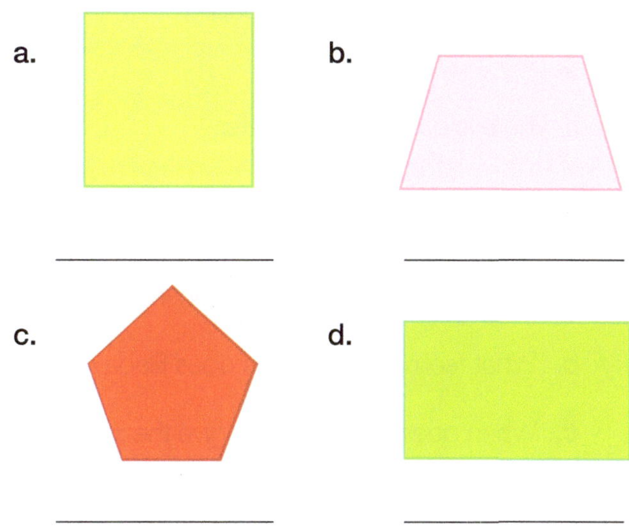

2. Draw and then count the diagonals in each polygon.

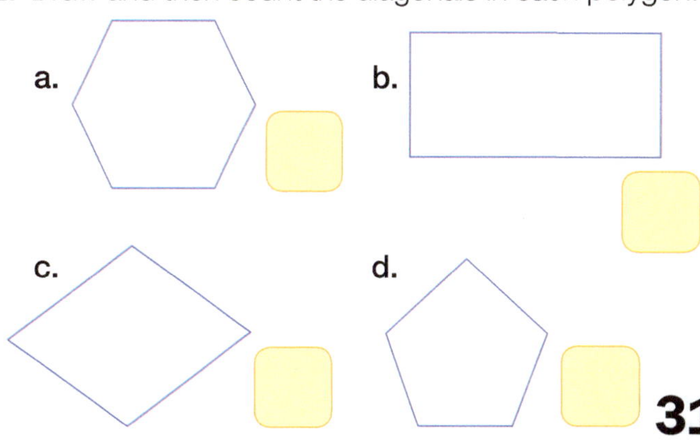

Letter to my Grandma

2736 Fair Weather Road
Forest Glen NSW 2897

11 July

Dear Baba,

I know it will be your birthday very soon and I want to be the first one to wish you a very happy birthday. I would love to visit you soon and bring you my present. I have made something for you but it's a surprise. I know you are going to be very pleased with it because I just love it. It took me a while to make but I did enjoy the time I spent putting everything together. I bet you can't guess what it is I made? No? And I am not going to spoil all the fun you will get when you see it by telling you what it is now. You will just have to wait until I can bring it over on my next visit.

Remember what you always tell me: It's not the gift but the thought that counts.

Anyway, I know you will love and cherish my gift as much as I love and cherish you. You always make me feel so special. You always make me happy and I know you are always pleased to see me when I visit. That's why I can't wait for my next visit and bring my birthday gift to you.

Cheers Baba. See you soon.

Love
Bec xxx

Understanding

Circle **T** (True) of **F** (False) to answer correctly

a. Bec wrote the letter to her Baba.	**T**	**F**	**b.** Baba is Bec's Grandma.	**T**	**F**
c. Baba is not an English expression.	**T**	**F**	**d.** Bec's birthday is near.	**T**	**F**
e. Bec made a present for Baba.	**T**	**F**	**f.** Grandma loves Bec very much.	**T**	**F**
g. Bec made Baba a rug.	**T**	**F**	**h.** Baba can't wait for her present.	**T**	**F**
i. There is a moral in this letter.	**T**	**F**	**j.** It's the gift that counts.	**T**	**F**

Interpreting

Write an answer to each question.

a. How does Bec always feel when she goes to visit Baba? ______________________

b. What feelings or qualities does Baba instil in Bec when she visits? ______________________

c. When does Bec intend to give the present to her grandma? ______________________

d. Describe how Bec feels about making the present. ______________________

e. What is the message about gift giving in Bec's letter?______________________

Grammar

Adjectives with **Suffixes** Y, FUL, OUS, ISH

Make adjectives from each noun using one of the suffixes above.

a. danger ______________ **b.** fame ______________ **c.** beauty ______________

d. ice ______________ **e.** dread ______________ **f.** self ______________

g. delight ______________ **h.** ease ______________ **i.** thick ______________

Spelling

Words with the same sound - 'oi' and 'oy'

enjoy, foil, toy, noise, voice, buoy, annoy, employ, coin, moist, destroy, spoil

Column A – oi words ______________________

Column B – oy words ______________________

Missing Letters Fill in the missing letters to complete the word in each sentence.

a. It will soon be Baba's b ___ ___ t h d ___ ___.

b. Bec made Baba a p r ___ s ___ n t.

c. She is very ___ ___ e a s ___ ___ with it.

d. R ___ ___ ___ ___ b ___ r to ___ ___ a p it.

Word Building

Add **'ing'** with blends to make new words.

a. st ____________

b. str ____________

c. sw ____________

d. wr ____________

e. br ____________

f. fl ____________

g. cl ____________

h. th ____________

Punctuation

Use the Exclamation Mark to Show Surprise or Give Commands.

Re-write each of the following correctly.

a. Wow ____________ **b.** Stop ____________ **c.** Quick March ____________

Equivalent Fractions

1. Write the shaded squares as a fraction.

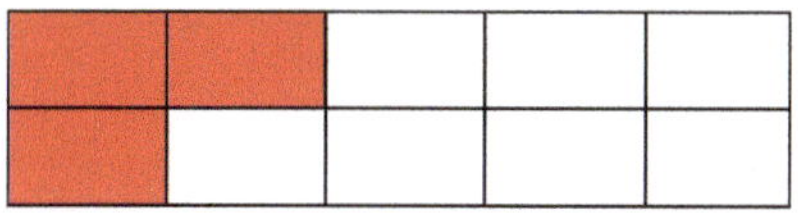

____

2. Add 5/8 and 2/8 = ________

3. Arrange these fractions in rising order.

$\frac{1}{2}$ $\frac{3}{10}$ $\frac{4}{5}$ $\frac{7}{10}$ $\frac{1}{5}$ $\frac{3}{5}$

4. Subtract these fractions. N.B. All have the same denominator.

a. $\frac{7}{8} - \frac{3}{8} =$ ☐ **b.** $\frac{3}{5} - \frac{2}{5} =$ ☐

c. $\frac{3}{4} - \frac{1}{4} =$ ☐ **d.** $\frac{7}{12} - \frac{5}{12} =$ ☐

5. Change the second fraction to an equivalent fraction then add.

a. $\frac{1}{4} + \frac{1}{2} =$ ☐ **b.** $\frac{1}{6} + \frac{2}{3} =$ ☐ **c.** $\frac{3}{10} + \frac{1}{2} =$ ☐

Decimals

1. Write each decimal on the number line.

0.3 1.2 0.8 1.1 0.5

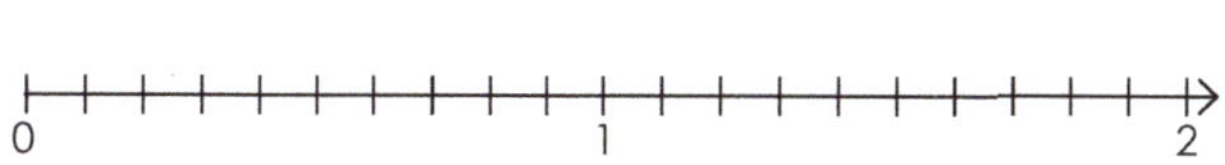

0.9 0.7 1.6 1.9 0.4

2. Write the missing middle fraction in each pattern.

a. 0.4 ☐ 0.6 **b.** 2.4 ☐ 2.2

c. 1.5 ☐ 1.9 **d.** 0.9 ☐ 0.6

e. 0.8 ☐ 1.2 **f.** 1.5 ☐ 0.5

3. Fill in the missing decimals in each pattern.

0.1	0.2		0.4		0.6

4. Add these decimal fractions.

a. 1.3 + 1.9 = ________ **b.** 2.5 + 0.3 = ________

Lurking Danger

"They sat precariously on the rock ledge dangling their feet over the side.

The two mates enjoyed their trips away but this one was about to take a sudden and unexpected turn.

These are the first lines of Lurking Danger by Ty Blackcamp, no doubt intended from the outset to capture the reader's attention and interest. Suspense and excitement are conjured up at the very beginning to provide the reader with a powerful image that will capture their imagination, requiring at least a further look at this writing.

Set on the coastal terrain of north-east Australia it draws on the experience of two school friends who take off for a week-end trip in their old, beaten-up ute, which will be their sleeping quarters for the duration. The friends often go away together and their friendship is one built on their enjoyment of each other's company, their sense of adventure and their close affinity to the ocean.

Blackcamp takes the opportunity to share with his readers the extraordinary beauty of coastal Australia while drawing on the latest calamity to beset two good friends. He is able to paint the uncertainty and unpredictability of the ocean, its movement and tides and the traps awaiting the inexperienced and unprepared visitor while detailing how sudden movements in rock formations along the coastline can have dire consequences.

You will have to read the book to find out what happens to the two mates and how their week-end plans are thrown into disarray. At the same time you can enjoy the images of the Australian coastline which are interwoven throughout.

Understanding

Shade the bubble for the best answer

a. The closest meaning of 'conjured up'is

- ◯ painted images
- ◯ joined together
- ◯ brought to life
- ◯ written about

b. The best meaning of 'dire consequences' is

- ◯ sad results
- ◯ bad results
- ◯ uneasy results
- ◯ fearful results

c. Who is most likely to read this story?

- ◯ Mainly girls
- ◯ Mainly boys
- ◯ Mums and Dads
- ◯ Mainly boys and girls

d. What disaster befell the two friends?

- ◯ the movement of the coastline
- ◯ the movement of the tides
- ◯ traps awaiting the inexperienced
- ◯ the movement of the ocean

Interpreting

Write an answer to each question.

a. How did the two mates travel to the coast? ______________________

b. Where did the mates form their friendship? ______________________

c. Is this the first time these trips met with disaster? ______________________

d. Explain the basis of the boys' friendship. ______________________

e. Do you think this is a real book? Explain. ______________________

Grammar

Adjectives add meaning to Nouns. Write the adjective or adjectives in each sentence on the line.

a. The red shoes were worn by the ballet dancer. ______________________

b. Our new house will be ready by next month. ______________________

c. Dire consequences result from many different events. ______________________

d. The coastal terrain is always a wonderful sight to see. ______________________

Spelling

Plural of some nouns ending in **O** add **ES**
Write each word in its plural form.

a. tomato ____________ **b.** potato ____________

c. hero ____________ **d.** echo ____________

e. volcano ____________ **f.** mosquito____________

Some Nouns just add S to form the plural

g. avocado ____________ **h.** fiasco ____________

i. photo ____________ **j.** Kilo ____________

k. ratio ____________ **l.** video ____________

Proof Reading: Incorrect Spelling of Words
Cross out the word spelt incorrectly and write it correctly on the line.

a. It was so unperdiktable that no one paid atenshun to it ____________

b. The hole otein was extrodinary thruout the country. ____________

c. We often xpereence wonderfull advensers. ____________

Word Building

Synonyms – Word with like meaning

anger, brave, heal, mend, hidden, harsh

Match the words from the word bank to the given words.

a. concealed ____________

b. courageous ____________

c. fury ____________

d. cure ____________

e. repair ____________

f. cruel ____________

Punctuation

Quoted Speech in Broken Sentences.

Copy each sentence correctly. Watch the speech marks.

a. "Come quickly!" Dad called, "we have to catch the bus."

____

b. "Before long," Josie sighed, "it will be time for bed."

____

Measuring Angles

1. Circle the angle less than 60 degrees.

a. 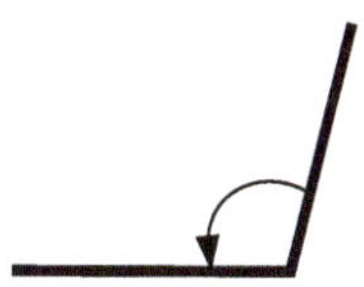

b. 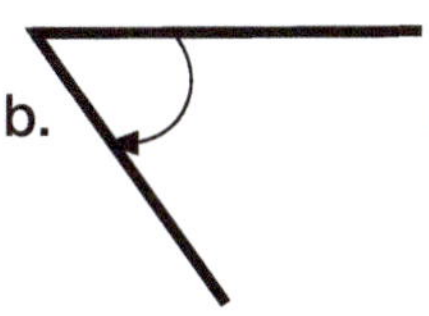

c. 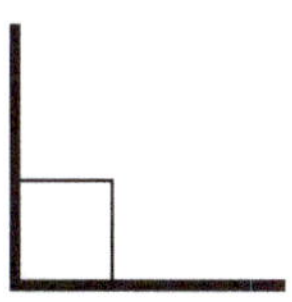

d. 

e. 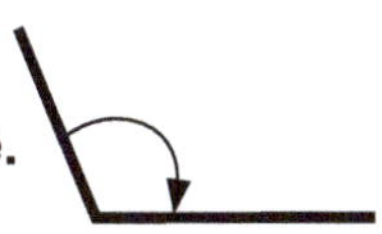

2. Write in degrees, the angle showing on each protractor.

a. 

____

b. 

____

3. Show each angle on the protractor.

a. 80°

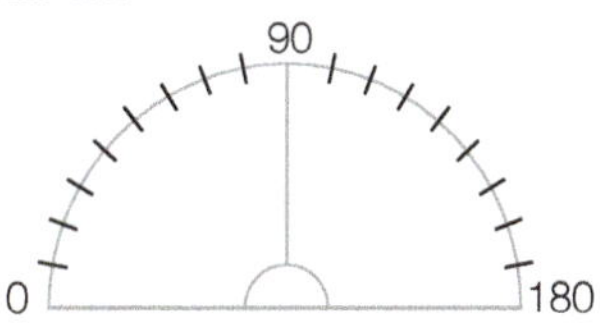

b. 130°

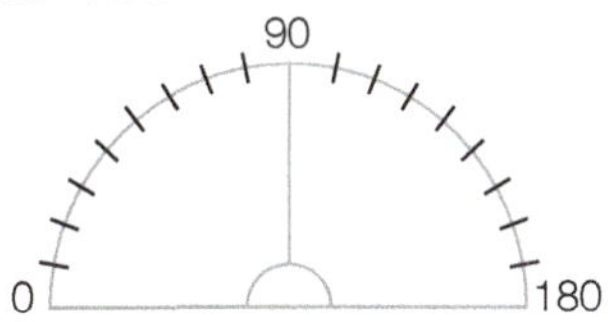

Line Graph

This line graph shows a bicycle journey for six hours. Use the graph to answer the questions.

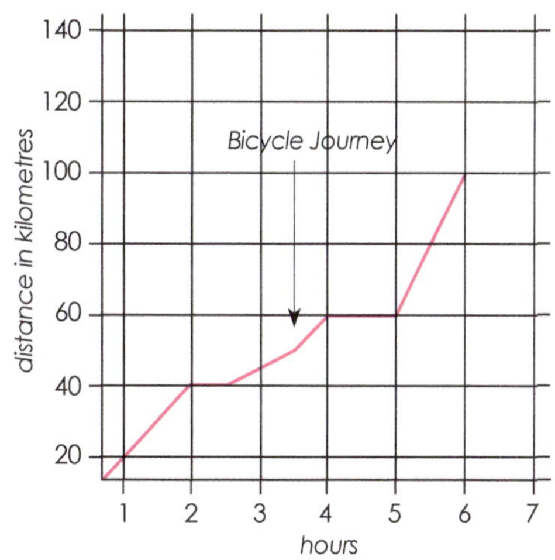

1. How far did the cyclist travel in the first two hours? ____________

2. If the cyclist left home at 7:00 am, what time was the first rest taken? ____________

3. How long was the first rest? ____________

4. How long did it take? ____________

5. What was the time when the cyclist reached 50 km from home? ____________

Australia - Its Discovery to Free Settlers

1606 Dutchman Willem Janszoon, sails along the coast of Terra Australis Incognita (unknown southern land).

1616 Dutchman Dirk Hartog, lands on the West Australian Coast, just north of Shark Bay.

1642 Dutch explorer, Abel Tasman discovers Van Deimen's Land, now called Tasmania.

He is a mariner with the Dutch East Indies Company. Australia is known as New Holland.

1770 Englishman, Lieutenant James Cook sails HM Barque Endeavour along the east coast of Australia.

Charts the east coast for Britain and names New South Wales.

King George III is the reigning monarch.

1778 Captain Arthur Phillip and the First Fleet arrives in Botany Bay between 18 – 20 January but moves to Sydney Cove, in Port Jackson, on 26 January 1788. This day is now celebrated as Australia Day each year. The First Fleet is met by the Cadigal people, the first settlers of this area of land.

1790 The Second Fleet of convicts arrives in Sydney Cove.

1791 The Third Fleet of convicts arrives and in

1793 The first free settlers arrive in NSW.

Understanding

Write the date for each event.

a. King George III is King of England. ____________

b. White man arrives in Sydney Cove. ____________

c. The Dutch first sight Australia. ____________

d. Free settlers arrive in NSW ____________

e. The First Fleet arrives at Botany Bay ____________

f. The Dutch land in Western Australia. ____________

g. Australia Day is celebrated on ____________

h. Australia is the unknown southern land. ____________

i. The arrival of the Second Fleet ____________

j. Abel Tasman discovers Tasmania. ____________

Interpreting

Match a word to its meaning.

Dutch, Gadigal, Unknown Land, Mariner, Free Settlers, Reigning Monarch

a. An Aboriginal Tribe ____________________

b. Present King or Queen. ____________________

c. One who sails the seas ____________________

d. terra incognita ____________________

e. Able to choose where to go ____________________

f. Coming from Holland ____________________

Grammar

Adjectives to Identify Distance in Time and Space

Singular = **this** (near) and **that** (afar) **Plural** = **these** (near) and **those** (afar)

Circle the correct word in brackets to correctly complete each sentence.

a. May we have (this/those) pencil or (that/these) one?

b. (Those/These) houses are built from timber compared to (those/this).

c. Take care of (this/these) shoes because (this/those) is the last pair in the shop.

d. How far is (this/that) school for you to travel on (this/that) bus?

e. Will (that/those) girls be able to come to (this/these) house for (this/these) party?

Spelling

Homophones - Same sound, different spelling and different meaning. Write the meaning of each word on the line.

a. choose ______________ **b.** chews ______________

c. boar ______________ **d.** bore ______________

Use each word correctly.

e. The old ______________ will go to market this week.

f. You need to ______________ what to do.

g. The cow ______________ its cud all day.

h. We have ______________ water on the farm.

Proof Reading: Cross out incorrect words and write them correctly.

a. In 1606 marriners from Europe sailed the waters of the coast of our land. ______________

b. Between 1606 and 1788 marriners from diffrent nations visited out waters. ______________

c. Merchent ships from the Dutch East Indees Company sailed along our coast. ______________

d. In 1770, the Englishmen Lutenant James Cook, sailed the east coast. ______________

Word Building

Nominalisation - Making Nouns from Verbs. Write each verb as a noun.

a. inform ______________

b. courageous ______________

c. classify ______________

d. support ______________

e. notify ______________

f. describe ______________

Punctuation

Using an **Ellipsis** for Omission, Suspense or Time Delay.

Identify how the ellipsis is used in each example. Write O, S or TD on the line.

a. We left late … ______________ **b.** Then the road opened … ______________

c. What will they do … ______________ **d.** No way … we can't. ______________

Location

1. Find streets and landmarks on this road map. Use the given co-ordinates to locate and write them.

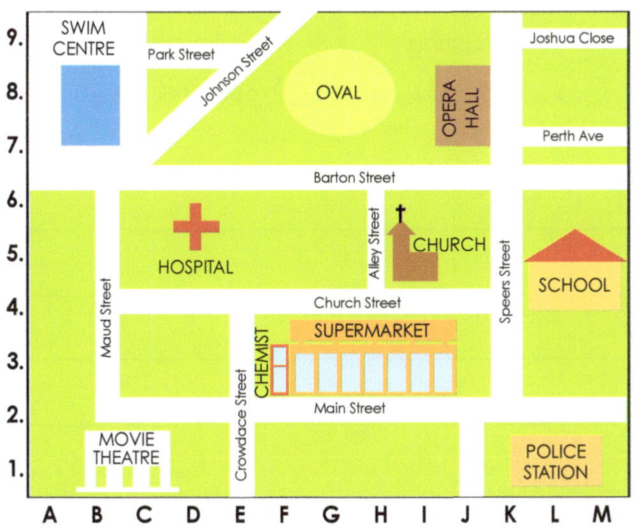

a. B8 ______________ **b.** B6 ______________

c. L4 ______________ **d.** J2 ______________

e. D5 ______________ **f.** H3 ______________

g. J5 ______________ **h.** F3 ______________

i. L9 ______________ **j.** L1 ______________

k. G7 ______________ **l.** J8 ______________

Ordering Time

1. Order each activity from the earliest to the latest time, using the times provided.

9am, 1pm, 7am, 7:15am, 11am, 6:30pm, 9:30pm, 3pm, 8am, 4:30pm

a. Eat lunch at school. ______________

b. Get up in the morning. ______________

c. Do my homework. ______________

d. School begins. ______________

e. Eat dinner with the family. ______________

f. Enjoy my recess break. ______________

g. Leave for school. ______________

h. Go to bed. ______________

i. Have my breakfast. ______________

j. School finishes for the day. ______________

2. Write the alphabetical order of events - earliest to latest - beginning with 'b'

____

Discussion

Shopping with the Girls

Wow! We were free at last to meet up with our friends for a shopping expedition. We had planned to go early to avoid the huge crowds expected at the opening of our new shopping centre. It will be a big change for our district and is sure to be popular particularly when school is out.

Can you believe it? We are so excited that all of us have agreed to catch the eight thirty bus to be at our destination as soon as the shops open for trading. We will need to wear easy walkers because we intend to spend the whole day just exploring what is now available to buy that we haven't had easy access to before. In these large shopping complexes there are usually plenty of places where good quality shoes, bags and clothes can be found. There are also opportunities to purchase nice bling and cosmetics at a reasonable price. Something that will not use all our spending money in one go. Boy! We can hardly wait.

Also, there should be plenty of different cuisines to tempt the hungry. We expect there will be the usual traders in the Food Hall but we are hoping there will be some who will tempt us to try something different and which hasn't been previously available. As long as it is not too expensive we should be able to share a plate or two with each other, of different dishes, just to get a taste for what could become a regular treat.

Of course we are not going to spend all day shopping because this new centre has a cinema with some recent films on show. That is where we can go to rest up for an hour or two after all the exploring, buying and eating we have done.

We intend to make it a most enjoyable and memorable opening day.

Understanding

Shade the bubble for the best answer

a. A synonym for *cuisine* is

- ◯ styles
- ◯ traders
- ◯ foods
- ◯ tastes

b. The girls intend to catch

- ◯ a train
- ◯ a late bus
- ◯ a tram
- ◯ an early bus

c. They will go to the cinema to

- ◯ rest
- ◯ sleep
- ◯ shop
- ◯ eat

d. The day will be remembered as

- ◯ exhausting
- ◯ enjoyable
- ◯ successful
- ◯ surprising

Interpreting

Write an answer to each question.

a. To what does the 'it' in the fourth sentence refer? ______________________

b. Why are the girls so excited? ______________________

c. How long will the girls spend shopping? ______________________

d. Name two items mentioned that the girls might buy.______________________

e. Where might the group go to have a break? ______________________

Grammar

Relating Verbs in the Present Tense – am, is, are

Use the correct verb in each sentence.

a. They ____________ coming shopping with us.

b. Mum ____________ meeting us at the bus stop.

c. Harry and Bella ____________ away today.

d. I ____________ not going to the school assembly.

e. You ____________ not going swimming now.

f. It ____________ raining heavily outside tonight.

Cross out the incorrect verb in each sentence.

a. You (is/are) going to be in the team.

b. She (is/are) having a birthday party tomorrow.

c. The girls (is/are) going shopping today.

d. There (is/am/are) a lot of food left over tonight.

Spelling

Rule – **'ck'** only follows a short vowel and sounds like 'k'
Add the consonants to form words. Write the word.

a. c r i ___ e t ________ **b.** b u ___ e t ________
c. r o ___ e t ________ **d.** h e ___ l e ________
e. c r a ___ e r ________ **f.** s p r o ___ e t ________

Form **word opposites** using the prefix **'un'**.

a. friendly ________ **b.** comfortable ________
c. seen ________ **d.** certain ________
e. fortunate ________ **f.** kind ________

Syllabification: Write each word in syllables

a. cinema ________ **b.** cuisine ________
c. available ________ **d.** expedition ________
e. destination ________

Word Building

Use the blends spr and str with the endings – ay, ing, ain. ingy

a. ________
b. ________
c. ________
d. ________
e. ________
f. ________
g. ________
h. ________

Punctuation

Abbreviations – With **NO** Full Stops

Write the abbreviation for each group of words. One is done for you.

a. Royal Australian Navy = RAN **b.** Victoria Cross ________ **c.** Post Office ________
d. Australian Capital Territory ________ **e.** New South Wales ________ **f.** Governor General ________

Distance

1. Use the scaled map to complete the activities.

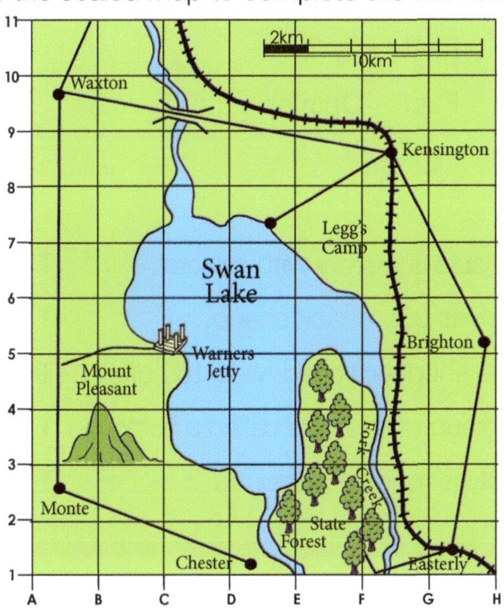

a. In which direction is Monte from Chester? ________
b. Which town is north of Monte? ________
c. What is the distance from Brighton to Kensington? ________
d. Give the co-ordinates for the bridge between Kensington and Waxton. ________
e. In what direction does the railway run to Easterly. ________
f. What is the distance between Monte and Waxton? ________

Fractions

1. Here is a pie graph showing sports children like to play.

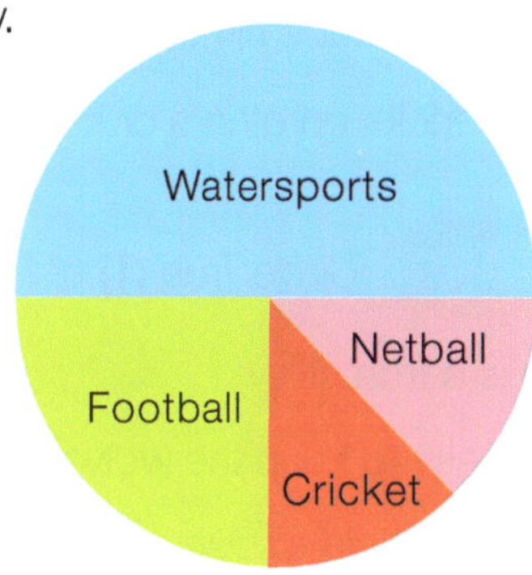

a. What is the most popular sport?
____
b. What percentage of children like to play water sports? ________
c. What percentage like football? ________
d. What two sports are liked equally?
____
e. If 40 children were surveyed, how many like to play football? ________
f. How many play netball? ________
g. How many play cricket? ________

The Boy Who Cried Wolf

This is a very old fable. It is about a boy who was a shepherd and a pack of wolves that roamed the hills and killed the sheep in his care.

Once upon a time a group of shepherds found it hard to look after their sheep and protect them from the wolves. These wolves had taken quite a toll on their flock so they decided to meet and develop a strategy to foil the wolves. If one of them spotted a wolf in the shadows he was to make a noise, throw clubs at the wolf and cry out, "Wolf, Wolf!" then the others would come running to help frighten the animals away.

Now, one shepherd boy thought it would be a funny joke if he cried, "Wolf, Wolf!" during the night when the others were asleep. And, so he did. But when the other shepherds came and found they had been brought from their beds by a joking shepherd they were angry and shook their firsts at the prankster. But, the silly boy did not learn his lesson and so he used his stunt again the next night and still his friends came to his aid. But, alas! There was no wolf in sight.

Unfortunately, a couple of nights later a pack of wolves really did attack the young shepherd's flock. He began to panic and cried as loud as he could, "Wolf, Wolf!". But the other shepherds did not want to be made to look foolish again so they rolled over and went back to sleep. No one came to help the shepherd boy that night and he lost all his sheep. He had cried wolf once too often just for the fun of it and when he really needed help no one answered his cry for help.

So the moral of this story is don't play silly pranks on your friends because when you really need help no one might believe you and come to help you.

Understanding

Circle if each statement is a **Fact** or an **Opinion**.

a. The shepherd was a silly person. Fact Opinion

b. Other Shepherds were annoyed with the prankster. Fact Opinion

c. The moral in this story is clear to see. Fact Opinion

d. The prankster made himself look foolish. Fact Opinion

e. Don't play tricks on others or it could backfire! Fact Opinion

Interpreting

Circle True (T) or False (F) to answer correctly.

a. This fable is a true story. T F

b. A Fable is a story with a moral. T F

c. It was not easy to keep the wolves at bay. T F

d. Wolves only attack sheep. T F

e. A meeting was held to discuss the problem. T F

f. One shepherd cried 'wolf' too often. T F

g. No one came to help when really needed. T F

h. A group of sheep is called a flock. T F

i. The lookout was not believed by the others. T F

j. Wolves roam in packs. T F

Grammar

Collective Nouns Match the collective nouns with their relative expressions.

herd, flock, swarm, choir, school, fleet, pack, team, audience, congregation

a. People at a concert ____________

b. A number of bees ____________

c. A number of fish ____________

d. A number of ships ____________

e. People in church ____________

f. A number of sheep ____________

g. A number of wolves ____________

h. A number of cattle ____________

i. A number of singers ____________

j. A group of players ____________

Spelling

Words ending in a vowel and 'l' double the 'l' when a suffix is added.
Eg., travel = travelled. Write new words. Add 'ed', 'ing', and 'er' to each word.

a. quarrel ______ ______ ______

b. travel ______ ______ ______

c. marvel ______ ______ ______

d. propel ______ ______ ______

Proof Reading: Inverted Commas and Correct Spelling.
Place inverted commas around the spoken words. Cross out the wrong words and spell them correctly.

a. Whn will tee be ready? arst Jim. ______

b. Do you wont to go swiming with me? ______

c. Their is a lot of homewerk tonight kried Josie. ______

d. It was neerly dark when mum cauled evrywon come to dinner.

______

Word Building

Build new words using the blend 'cr' and these endings.

ENDINGS: itical, iticise, eepy, umble, ony, ucial, uise, usade

a. ______

b. ______

c. ______

d. ______

e. ______

f. ______

g. ______

h. ______

Punctuation

Capital Letters and **Full Stops** and **Personal Pronoun 'I'**

Re-write the following sentences using correct punctuation where needed.

the shepherd played silly pranks on other shepherds they were very cross with him and i think i would be too what do you think

______

______

Volume

1. Count the one centimetre cubes in each model to find its volume.

a. 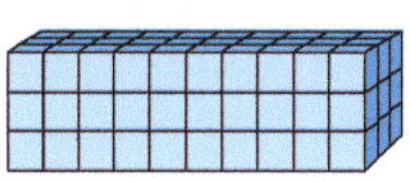

[ ] cm^3

b. 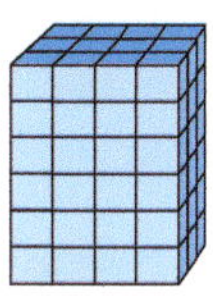

[ ] cm^3

c. 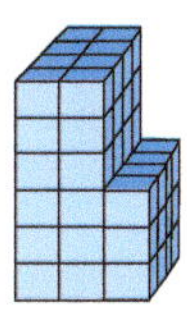

[ ] cm^3

2. Use the formula, length x height x depth, (**L x H x D**) to find the volume of each model.

a. 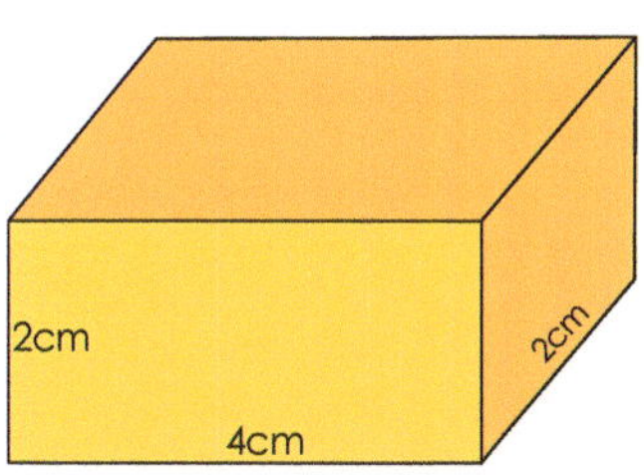

L x H x D = V

___ x ___ x ___ = ___

Volume = ______ cm^3

b. 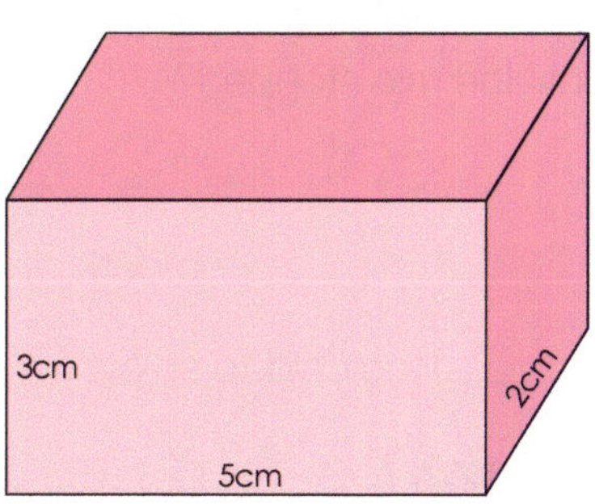

L x H x D

___ x ___ x ___

Volume = ______ cm^3

Chance

1. Roll a die to achieve a specific number.

Roll 3	Tally	Total

Roll 6	Tally	Total

2. Write the fraction to express the chance of landing on the given number.

a. 

4 = [ ]

b. 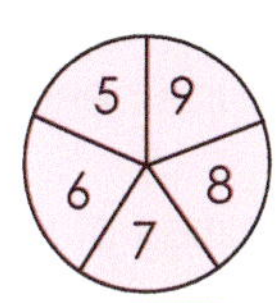

8 = [ ]

c. 

2 = [ ]

d. 

5 = [ ]

e. 

3 = [ ]

f. 

12 = [ ]

3. Answer either, **possible** OR **impossible**, for each statement.

a. Mum will win lotto tonight ______

b. I can roll a seven on a die. ______

c. Toss two coins and both will land on heads. ______

How to Arrange Groups

Explanation

Groups are a great way to get people organised for doing jobs and planning activities as well as sharing the amount of work each one has to do for a successful outcome.

First of all decide how many people would be suitable for each group to succeed. Then identify who works well together, and who has the ability to lead the group. Then each person should identify what it is they are good at and how, as well as with whom, they can work, to achieve success.

Next, the group or groups need to select their leader. This person should be someone who is able to get on with all members in the group, be fair and give everyone a go. They might already have had leadership experience in other groups or show leadership potential. Some leaders are born to the role while others have to develop leadership skills over time.

Once the structure of the group is settled each member of the group needs to identify what skills they bring to help achieve the group's task. Give each member an opportunity to express their own strengths and weaknesses and how each one can assist and support others in the group. Most members will know their own limitations and what they can and can't do. Then it will depend on how well the leader delegates responsibilities to each member for the group to be cohesive and successful.

Remember, the whole idea of working in groups is for everyone to be actively involved, to share the 'heavy lifting' and 'lighten the load' for everyone. Full participation in a group will benefit the whole group and assist it to achieve its purpose and goals.

Understanding

Shade the bubble for the best answer.

a. What is the purpose of this text?

- ◯ to inform
- ◯ to sell
- ◯ to retell
- ◯ to argue

b. How should groups be formed?

- ◯ by the teacher
- ◯ by its members
- ◯ by parents
- ◯ by the principal

c. Which statement is true?

- ◯ Group members need no skills
- ◯ Teachers should form the groups.
- ◯ All groups should elect their leader
- ◯ Groups make it hard to get things done

d. Which statement is false?

- ◯ group members have many skills
- ◯ group members need to work alone
- ◯ group leaders delegate responsibilities
- ◯ groups work together for a common purpose.

Interpreting

Write an answer to each question.

a. What qualities are needed by members of a group? ____________________

b. How can groups benefit their members? ____________________

c. Write the qualities of a good leader. ____________________

d. What is meant by 'heavy lifting'? ____________________

Grammar

Relating Verbs in the Past Tense - was, were

Cross out the incorrect verb in each sentence.

a. Yesterday (were/was) Wednesday and tomorrow (were/is) Thursday.

b. We (was/were) at cricket practice when it started to rain. Where (was/were) you?

c. (Was/were) the boys very wet or (was/were) they able to find good cover until the rain stopped?

Use the correct verb in each sentence.

a. Before long they ______________ able to drive home before it ______________ too dark.

b. Mum and I ______________ going to the beach before it ______________ too cold to enjoy.

c. Do you know where the beach is or ______________ you unable to find it easily?

Spelling

Plural of Nouns ending in f, fe or if change the f to v before adding es.
Write each word in the plural.

a. knife ______ **b.** wife ______ **c.** life ______

d. wolf ______ **e.** shelf ______ **f.** half ______

g. loaf ______ **h.** thief ______ **i.** leaf ______

Other words ending in f or ff simply add s.

a. roof ______ **b.** dwarf ______ **c.** chef ______

NOTE: These words allow both plurals.
wharf - wharfs, wharves   hoof - hoofs, hooves   scarf - scarfs, scarves

Proof Reading: Correct the spelling error in each sentence.
Write the new word on the line.

a. The wolfs were roaming in a pack. ______

b. Those rooves are rusty. ______

c. The seven dwarves stole the show. ______

d. Their wifes are out shopping. ______

Word Building

Write a **synonym** for each word from the text.

a. benefit ______

b. team ______

c. leader ______

d. limitation ______

e. delegate ______

f. goal ______

Punctuation

The Hyphen – A short stroke

Here are examples of its use with compound words, as an inclusive function, as a stutter or for spelling.

Ice-cream   *June - July*   *1938 - 1945*   *W-w-what?*   *d-r-e-a-m*

Underline and place the hyphen where it should be used in these sentences.

The period between 1914 1918 usually denotes the First World War whereas the Second World War is marked from 1939 1945. Both wars began about May June and August September .

Show how you would spell this word using the hyphen: responsibilities ______

Factors

1. Multiply the factors to find the product.

a. 6 x 7 = ☐   **b.** 4 x 8 = ☐

c. 8 x 3 = ☐   **d.** 5 x 7 = ☐

e. 9 x 6 = ☐   **f.** 6 x 4 = ☐

g. 7 x 8 = ☐   **h.** 3 x 11 = ☐

2. Answer True (T) or (F) for each statement about factors.

a. 7 is a factor of sixty-three ☐

b. 9 is a factor of eighty-one ☐

c. 6 is a factor of forty-four ☐

d. 5 is a factor of sixty-five ☐

e. 4 is a factor of eighty-six ☐

f. 8 is a factor of seventy-two ☐

Multiplication

1. Use the contracted form to find the product for each of these.

a. 534 / 2 x ______

b. 327 / 3 x ______

c. 126 / 4 x ______

d. 464 / 2 x ______

e. 137 / 5 x ______

f. 405 / 6 x ______

2. Write the missing product on the wheel.

a.

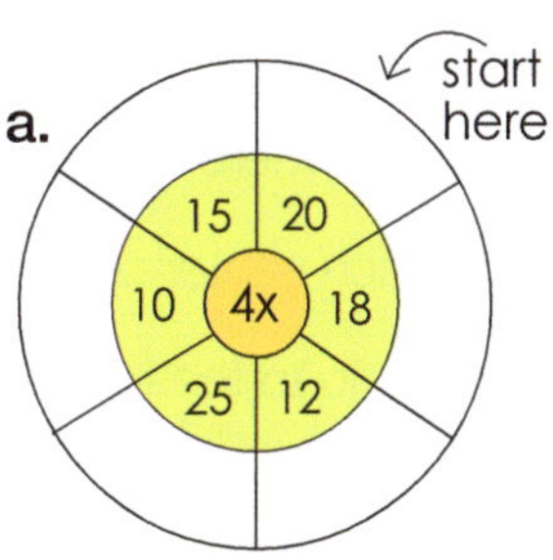

b.

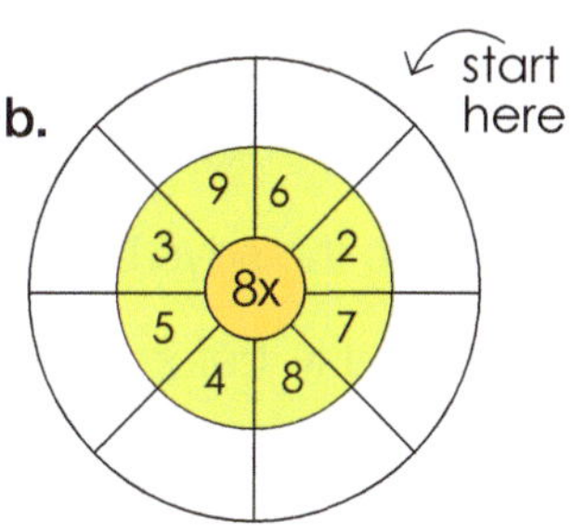

3. a. What is the capacity of 4 cans of soft drink if each can holds 375 mL?

______ x
______

Foreign Greetings and Farewells

Here are some common expressions in different languages. See if you can read and pronounce them too. Get an adult to help you with the pronunciation. Look at their similarities and hear them too.

ENGLISH	GERMAN	FRENCH	ITALIAN
Good morning	Guten morgan	Bonjour	Buon gjorno
Good night	Gate nacht	Bon Nute	Buona notté
Thank you	Danke	Merci	Grazie
Good bye	Auf wiederseden	Au revoir	Arrivederci
Hi	Hallo	Salut / Allo	Ciao

Understanding

Write an answer to each question.

a. Which language sounds similar to words in English? ____________________

b. What are the languages that sound most alike? ____________________

c. How is 'thank you' said in French? ____________________

d. Which language do you think 'mon amie' is? ____________________

e. What do you think 'Amigo' means? ____________________

Interpreting

Use the following languages correctly in the sentences.

merci beaucoup, arrivederci, danke, gutten morgan, good bye

a. The lady bought fruit at the shop and said ____________ to the shopkeeper.

b. After the party we left to go home and wished everyone ____________.

c. I said ____________ to show my mother how grateful I was for the present.

d. The children said ____________ to their teacher.

e. "____________ Roma" was a well-known song in the 1960s.

Grammar

Adverbial Phrases – Phrases do **NOT** have a verb.

Remember – Adverbs tell how, when, where or why.

underline the adverbial phrases in each sentence.

a. Today, before school, I had to go to the butchers for mum.

b. After recess, we had School Assembly to farewell Year 6.

c. By lunch time the rain had started and it was too heavy for afternoon sport.

d. In the afternoon we are going home with our mates, on the bus, for his party.

e. This evening there will be a meeting at the hall to discuss the new bridge over the river.

Spelling

Root Words – Octo from the Latin meaning eight.

Find the meaning of the following words and write each one on the line.

a. octopus ____________________

b. octave ____________________

c. octogenarian ____________________

d. octagon ____________________

Why was **October** the eighth month of the year? ____________________

Dictionary Practice: Write these words in Alphabetical Order.
octopus, octave, octagon, octogenarian, October, octet, occult, ochre

a.__________ b.__________ c.__________

d.__________ e.__________ f.__________ g.__________ h.__________

Word Building

The **suffix 'ion'** means 'the act of'. It might be written as 'tion' or 'sion'

Use these meanings and write the 'ion' word.

a. moving forward pr__________

b. multiplying numbers m__________

c. dividing numbers d__________

d. stretching or straining t__________

e. exploring a region ex__________

f. making up one's mind d__________

Punctuation

Commas in Lists and Phrases.

Insert the missing commas in each sentence. Remember there is no comma before 'and'

a. We have a red brown green yellow and white flag on our car.

b. There will be cakes fruit lollies sausage rolls and yes there will be all kinds of drinks at the party.

c. Before tomorrow we must have all our work done and it has to be well written neat and tidy.

d. The Christmas Club gives us a chance to save for toys food gifts food hampers and much more.

e. On our overseas trip we will visit Turkey Greece Italy Germany Austria Spain and Great Britain.

Using A Calculator

1. Use the M+ button to add each calculation and the MR to total the separate operations.

a. 6 x 3 M+
+ 5 x 4 M+
+ 2 x 6 M+
MR ______

b. 8 x 5 M+
+ 7 x 3 M+
+ 6 x 6 M+
MR ______

c. 4 x 3 M+
+ 6 x 5 M+
+ 4 x 9 M+
MR ______

2. Do each horizontal addition using M+ and MR

a. 5 x 4 + 7 x 3 + 6 x 5 = ______

b. 3 x 9 + 5 x 8 + 7 x 8 = ______

c. 8 x 9 + 5 x 7 + 2 x 9 = ______

d. 7 x 7 + 6 x 9 + 8 x 9 = ______

3. Use a calculator to find the next 2 numbers in each pattern.

x4	7	28	112		
+26	2	28	54		
÷2	128	64	32		

Time

1. Find the total of each money sum.

a. $27.64
$18.37
+$15.89
$ ______

b. $48.32
$59.68
+$38.95
$ ______

c. $72.59
$87.88
+$69.77
$ ______

2. Problems:
Year 5 had three cake stalls.
The takings at each stall were $58.95, $126.80 and $79.35.
How much was taken altogether? ______

Total for the stalls $ ______

3. Find the missing numbers in each addition.

a. 6 378
4 ☐93
+2 646
13 3☐7

b. 4 538
6 ☐17
+5 429
16 88☐

c. 2 475
1 767
+3 ☐89
7 8☐1

How to Make a Caramel Slice

You can make this easy slice with no baking needed.

Ingredients:

250g plain, sweet biscuits
(You could use rice bubbles)

1 cup slivered almonds

125g butter

1 tin prepared caramel fill

TOPPING

200g chopped, dark chocolate

1 tablespoon vegetable oil

1. Lightly grease and line an 18 x 28cm slice tin
2. Finely crush the biscuits
3. Mix biscuits and almonds together on medium, in microwave for 30
4. Melt butter and add to biscuit mix seconds or until smooth when stirred.
5. Press mixture firmly over base of tin
6. Add caramel mix on top of biscuit mix

TOPPING

1. Melt chocolate in heatproof bowl,
2. Stir in the oil
3. Pour over biscuit mix and tilt to spread.

Chill until set then cut into squares.
Keep in airtight container, in fridge.

Understanding

Order these instructions correctly.

a. Pour chocolate topping over the caramel	☐	**b.** Crush the biscuits	☐
c. Add melted butter to the biscuits	☐	**d.** Prepare a tin for the slice	☐
e. Almonds and biscuits are mixed together	☐	**f.** Stir oil into the melted chocolate	☐
g. Use a tin of prepared caramel mix	☐	**h.** Chop the dark chocolate	☐

Interpreting

Circle **Yes** or **No** to answer each question.

a. Will you need an adult to help you make this slice?	**Yes**	**No**
b. Are the ingredients for this slice in your kitchen pantry?	**Yes**	**No**
c. Can this slice be made a few days before use?	**Yes**	**No**
d. Does this slice need time to set before cutting it?	**Yes**	**No**
e. Can the chocolate burn in the microwave?	**Yes**	**No**

Grammar

Present Participles and Helping Verbs

Insert the correct helping verb and present participle to make each sentence correct.

am going   was helping   is running   were racing   are singing

a. The boy and his family ______________________ in the long-distance race at the carnival.

b. Did you say they ______________________ at the Showground this afternoon?

c. Before too much longer I ______________________ on annual leave.

d. The whole school ______________________ with the car wash last week end.

e. All students in Year 5 ______________________ the National Anthem at the games.

Spelling

Homographs – Same Spelling with Different Meaning and Pronunciation

tear and tear   bow and bow   fare and fare

Match the word to its meaning.

a. A looped knot ______________ **b.** Charge for travel ______________

c. To pull apart ______________ **d.** To bend over ______________

e. Fine food ______________ **f.** A water droplet ______________

Missing Letters: Use the recipe to complete each word.

a. c h __ c __ l __ t __ **b.** s l __ v __ r __ d

c. t __ b l __ s p __ __ n **d.** c __ n t __ __ n __ r

e. __ __ r t __ g h t **f.** v __ g __ t __ b l __

g. What type of letters are missing? ______________

Word Building

Silent 'e' at the end of Words

Add the letter 'a' to each word then say the word aloud. There is no 'e' sound at the end of the word.

a. f __ m e **b.** l __ t e

c. m __ t e **d.** gr __ c e

e. s h __ m e **f.** f r __ m e

g. t r __ c e **h.** s h __ m e

i. b r __ k e

Punctuation

Quotation Marks Write each sentence with the correct punctuation marks.

a. hurry up cried dad ______________

b. the teacher asked has everyone finished ______________

c. i will be late said dom so don't wait up ______________

d. why has the bell rung early asked najib ______________

Area

1. Write the most appropriate unit of area for each shape. (m^2, ha or km^2).

a.

b.

2. Complete each statement to make it true.

a. ________ ha=km^2 **b.** 3ha= ________ m^2

c. 8 000m^2= ________ ha **d.** 900ha= ________ km^2

3. Use the scale 1cm = 20m to find the perimeter and area of each shape.

a.

Perimeter ________

Area ________

b.

Perimeter ________

Area ________

Subtraction

1. Using the contracted form, find the difference between the numbers.

a. 6 425 − 1 113 = ____	**b.** 8 679 − 4 257 = ____	**c.** 3 977 − 1 726 = ____
d. 8 751 − 2 437 = ____	**e.** 9 684 − 2 369 = ____	**f.** 5 637 − 1 488 = ____

2. Problems:

a. The local High School has 1 248 students. 289 Year 7 students went on an excursion. How many students were left at school?

- ________

____

3. Subtract to find the missing numbers.

a. 3 ☐ 1 6 − 1 433 = 2 2 ☐ 3	**b.** 4 8 ☐ 6 − 1 4 6 8 = 3 ☐ 5 8	**c.** 3 4 7 ☐ − 1 259 = 2 2 ☐ 3

Why I Should Learn to Read and Write

I believe it is so very important to be able to read and write if I am going to succeed in life. Of course what I mean by succeeding in life should be explained. I want to hold down a worthwhile position and earn a reasonable wage so I must learn the basic skills needed if I am to succeed in life. These skills will always depend on knowing and understanding language and being literate in that language. Basic skills for language learners are speaking, reading and writing.

There are individuals who know how to speak a language but have not had the opportunity to learn the mechanics of reading and writing in that language. Their progress and opportunities in life are restricted by limitations such as: not knowing how to tell the time; not understanding visual signs in the environment; not being able to read everyday notices, bus or train timetables, important letters, information disseminated to the community, and so on. These limitations restrict ones total involvement in society. The inability to read and write inhibits freedom to be independently involved in day-to-day living activities in a community. Just being able to complete basic forms, which are often required by service providers and government agencies, requires a certain level of literacy. There are still individuals who will need someone else to do these things for them because they cannot read and write.

Therefore, I need to understand how important it is to learn how to read and write. It will allow me to move beyond just an average job to a more satisfying position, with the ability to earn good money to support a quality lifestyle and participate fully in society. So I should learn these skills now in order to move ahead in the future and succeed in life!

Understanding

Shade the bubble for the best answer.

a. What are the basic skills needed to succeed in life? ______________________________

____

b. How do people without these basic skills manage? ______________________________

____

c. What is the meaning of the word 'literate'? ______________________________

____

d. Why is reading an important skill?______________________________

____

e. How can the lack of the basic skills hinder a person in life? ______________________________

____

Interpreting

Write the meaning of each word or group of words.

a. limitations ______________________ **b.** dissemination ______________________

c. inability ______________________ **d.** mechanics ______________________

e. service providers ______________________________

f. government agencies ______________________________

Grammar

Redundant Words (Not needed) Repeated Nouns and Pronouns

Cross out the noun, pronoun or noun group in bold and replace it with one pronoun.

Them we they she it

a. Paul and I love to drive cars. Paul and I (______________)are going to drive in the V8 races.

b. Drive these cars to the start. Drive these cars (______________)to the garage before the race starts.

c. Josie will be at the track early. Josie (______________) likes to get a ring-side seat at the track.

d. The car will need to be checked. The car (______________) must be in top condition for the race.

e. The Pit Crew are always the last to leave. The Pit Crew(______________) know their job is important.

Unit 23

Spelling

Drop the 'e' to some words when adding 'ing'
Re-write each word and add 'ing'

a. game ____________ b. come ____________
c. taste ____________ d. pursue ____________
e. inflate ____________ f. challenge ____________
g. queue ____________ h. glue ____________
i. change ____________

Dictionary Practice: Write 'before' or 'after' to make each one true.

a. dense comes __________ digit b. dream comes __________ dread
c. option comes __________ open d. record comes __________ recover
e. queen comes __________ queer f. knife comes __________ knave
g. dwell comes __________ dwarf h. leisure comes __________ lesion

Word Building

Use the Prefix **'anti'** to form new words meaning opposite or against.

climax, biotic, septic, dote,
clock-wise, social

a. ____________________
b. ____________________
c. ____________________
d. ____________________
e. ____________________
f. ____________________

Punctuation

Run-on Sentences

Re-write the following sentences correctly leaving out all unnecessary words.

a. The storm came in quickly. The storm was from the west and the storm created havoc.

____

b. They were waiting for a long time and then they could move and then they could take cover inside

____

Time

1. Write the digital time for each pm time.

a. 

b. 

c. 

d. 

e. 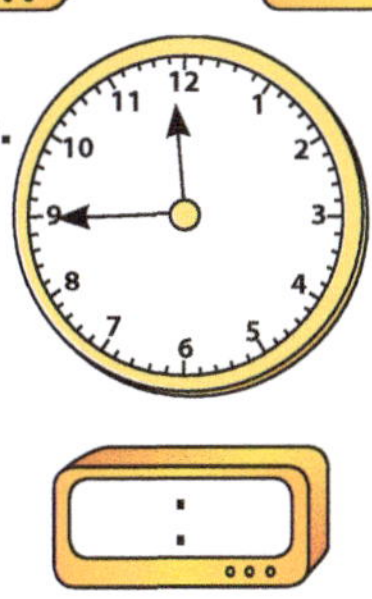

2. Write each time in words.

a. 7:30 ____________________
b. 14:25 ____________________
c. 16:15 ____________________
d. 23:45 ____________________
e. 00:01 ____________________

Multiplication

1. Complete each multiplication algorithm.

a. 27
34 x
______

b. 48
23 x
______

c. 42
36 x
______

d. 75
25 x
______

2. Use your knowledge of multiplication to complete the cross number puzzle.

Across	Down
1. 18 x 4 =	**1.** 2 x 36 =
3. 27 x 3 =	**2.** 2 x 7 =
5. 11 x 4 =	**4.** 2 x 9 =
6. 5 x 7 =	**6.** 4 x 8 =
9. 4 x 8 =	**7.** 7 x 9 =
11. 77 x 4 =	**8.** 6 x 5 =
	10. 7 x 4 =

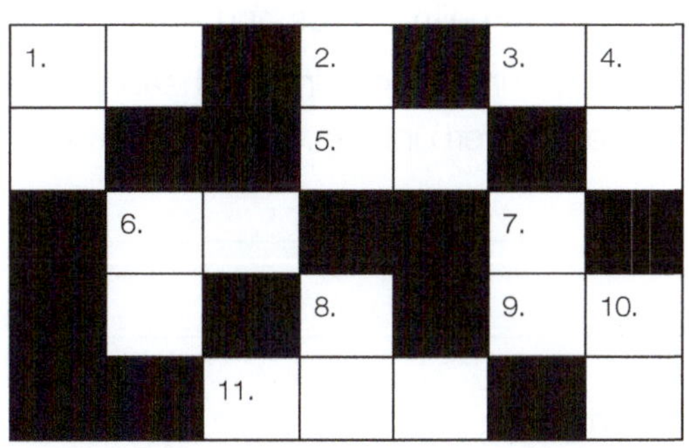

Understanding

Circle T (true) or F (False) to answer correctly.

a. The logo for this website has an owl in it. T F

b. These books can be ordered from this website. T F

c. There is a discount for ordering online. T F

d. You have access to a new catalogue on this website. T F

e. Some orders for these books can be delivered free of charge. T F

Interpreting

Write an answer to each question.

a. To whom would this website appeal? ______________________________

b. How do you know if this is a true representation of this website?

____

c. Who might be 'the distributor' and where might they be?

____

d. Write the address of this website. ______________________________

e. How many links are there on this website? ______________________________

Grammar

Feeling Verbs and Abstract Nouns

These verbs and nouns happen in your head you cannot see them. Eg. (to be) happy is happiness

Change each feeling verb into an abstract noun.

a. enjoy ______________ **b.** amuse ______________

c. please ______________ **d.** laugh ______________

e. delight ______________ **f.** irritate ______________

Spelling

Silent Letters 'k'- 'h' and 'g' to begin words. Write these words in alphabetical order.
gnome, knight, knave, knife, gnat, honour, honourable, knead, gnaw, honest, know, gnarled, honorary

____

____

Proof Reading: Circle the errors and write each word correctly.

a. The storm past overhead without much damige to the bildings.

____

b. Wen the rain stoped we went outside to sea the fludded street.

____

Word Building

Use the Prefix **'be'** to make new words
Write the new word with the prefix

a. cause ____________

b. fore ____________

c. come ____________

d. came ____________

Punctuation

Contractions are shortened words. Write the contracted words in each sentence, in full.

a. It's not going to rain tomorrow. ____________

b. We're going to play soccer. ____________

c. They're having a party tonight. ____________

d. You'll have to come home now. ____________

e. He should've gone to school. ____________

f. They won't be long either. ____________

Calculator and Patterns

1. Use your calculator to write the next three numbers in each pattern.

	Rule	Pattern
a.	x 3	4 132 ______ ______ ______
b.	+ 7	58 406 ______ ______ ______
c.	$\square^2$	25 ______ ______ ______
d.	+ 3 816	3 031 6 847 ______ ______ ______
e.	- 347	8 378 8 031 ______ ______ ______
f.	x 0.1	1 328 132.8 ______ ______ ______

2. Follow the path by calculating each step and fill in the missing numbers.

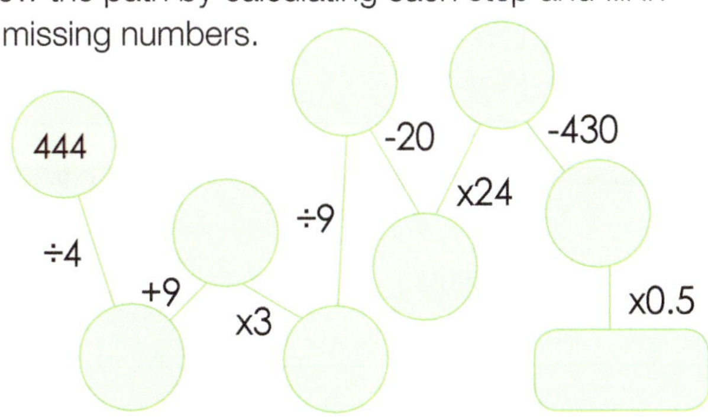

3. Multiply each decimal by 0.4

a. 24.3 ________ b. 35.6 ________ c. 8.07 ________

d. 0.95 ________ e. 17.66 ________ f. 2.83 ________

Equivalent Fractions

1. Colour the square in each that is not an equivalent fraction.

a.

$\frac{1}{2}$	$\frac{2}{10}$	0.5	50%

b.

$\frac{1}{4}$	0.25	$\frac{2}{8}$	25

c.

$\frac{2}{5}$	$\frac{4}{10}$	0.2	40%

d.

60%	6.0	$\frac{3}{5}$	$\frac{6}{10}$

e.

$\frac{3}{4}$	$\frac{1}{3}$	33%	0.333

f.

$\frac{3}{8}$	75%	$\frac{3}{4}$	0.75

2. Match the equivalent fraction to the correct diagram.

a.

b.
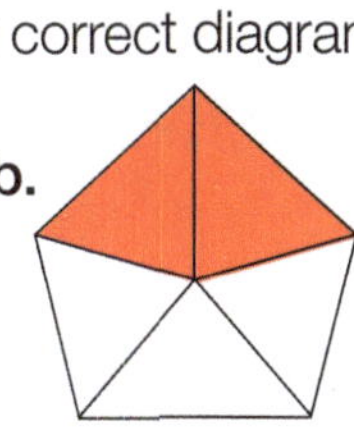

c.
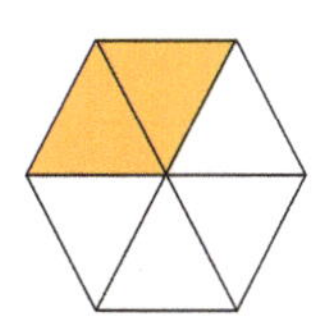

d.
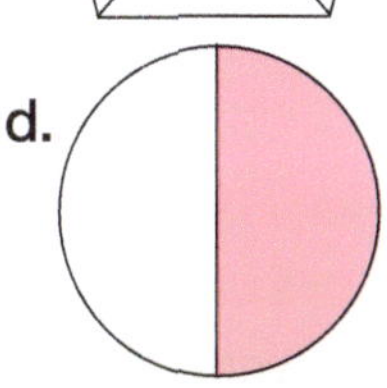

e.
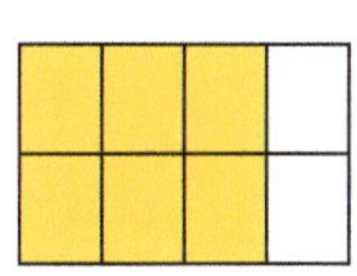

f.
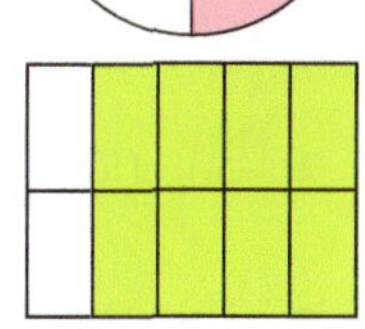

$\frac{1}{3}$

0.5

$\frac{4}{10}$

25%

$\frac{4}{5}$

75%

3. Write an equivalent fraction for each one.

a. $\frac{1}{2} = \frac{\square}{4}$ b. $\frac{4}{5} = \frac{\square}{10}$ c. $0.6 = \frac{\square}{5}$

Surfing Gear SALE

50-70% OFF

One Week Only

All items cost $40 and Under

Mens	Womens	Boys	Girls	Sale Clearance
T Shirts	Tops	Tees	Tops	Women's
Shorts	Bottoms	Swim Shorts	Rash Shirts	Boys
Footwear	Sandals	Thongs		Flip-Flops

Delivery Charges: Add $10 for all parcels

Purchase: Now using the following methods

Credit Card Debit Card Pay Wave

Phone Orders: 1300 123 456

Ring between 8:30am and 7:00pm Monday - Sunday

Fax: 1300 654 321 Email: wild@surfrider.com.au

www.surfrider.com.au

Understanding

Shade the bubble for the best answer.

a. How many options are there for paying?

- ◯ one
- ◯ two
- ◯ three
- ◯ four

b. What is this type of shopping called?

- ◯ in store
- ◯ on-line
- ◯ market stalls
- ◯ car boot

c. What types of items can be purchased?

- ◯ new
- ◯ old
- ◯ sale
- ◯ surf

d. Why would customers purchase online?

- ◯ convenience
- ◯ comfort
- ◯ style
- ◯ fashion

Interpreting

Write an answer to each question.

a. What do the words "now using" suggest for making a purchase?

____

b. How long will this sale last? ______________________________

c. Write the electronic address for this store. ______________________________

d. When are operators ready to assist you with a mail order?

____

e. What is different when you pay using a credit card and a debit card?

____

Grammar

Helping Verbs and the Future Tense

Re-write each sentence in the future tense – Eg., From He **sings** to He **will sing**.

a. She **rings** her brother every night. ______________________________

b. The children fell into the water. ______________________________

c. I grew a new rose this year. ______________________________

d. He came home late for lunch. ______________________________

Spelling

Homophones Circle the correct homophone in each sentence.

a. We (threw / through) a surprise party for my mother.

b. He put (flower / flour) in the cake.

c. The (rain / reign) of Queen Elizabeth II is very long.

d. We have very good (site / sight).

e. We will (lite / light) the fire when it's cold.

f. The (soul / sole) tastes very salty.

g. He was so (shore / sure) that he was correct.

h. Put (there / their) book over (there / their).

Word Building

Compound Words with **"Every"**
Add 'every' to each word to make new words.

a. body ____________

b. where ____________

c. thing ____________

d. one ____________

Alphabetical Order: Occupations Write these words in alphabetical order.
Look up the meaning of words you do not know.

dentist, chemist, florist, typist, pianist, artist, geologist, soloist, organist, prosthetist

____

____

Punctuation

Conjunctions (and, but, so, before, if, as, where, etc.) join phrases and clauses

Re-write these sentences as one using conjunctions. Leave out all redundant words.

a. We went to town for lunch. We went to town to shop. We went to town and we went to buy shoes.

____

b. Before long it was raining. Before long we looked for shelter. We could not find any.

____

Mass

1. Match each object to its correct mass.

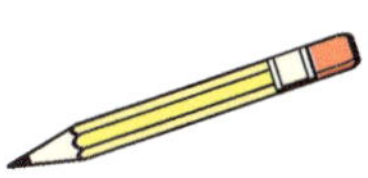

10g

2T

5kg

2kg

300kg

275g

3kg

45kg

2. Write each mass in its shortest form.

a. 3 000g ________ **b.** 4 500g ________

c. 10 200g ________ **d.** 6 500g ________

e. 8kg 500g ________ **f.** 10kg 250g ________

Division

1. Answer True (T) or False (F) for each statement.

a. 846 is a multiple of 6 ________ **b.** 5 is a factor of 90 ________

c. 93 is a multiple of 9 ________ **d.** 12 is a factor of 144 ________

e. 107 is a multiple of 7 ________ **f.** 8 is a factor of 60 ________

2. Complete each division in its contracted form.
Write the remainder too.

a. 8) 967 r

b. 4) 893 r

c. 5) 627 r

d. 4) 683 r

e. 9) 640 r

f. 7) 851

3. Find the missing number in each sentence.

a. ☐ ÷ 7 = 12 r 1

b. ☐ ÷ 5 = 16 r 2

Birdsong, Sweet!

Listen to that crisp, clean call of the butcher bird! Wow!

We can't help but think what wonderful attributes mother-nature has to share with mere mortals. It is no wonder we marvel at the sound of those different cries that are made daily for us humans to enjoy. The delightful sound they share with us is superb! Nothing can imitate those sounds so clearly, so accurately or so perfectly. We share in glorious birdsong without imitation or deceit, without fault and truly without compromise, freely, if we but listen. Just listen.

That is all this beautiful bird is asking and it will provide a wonderful symphony of sound in its dulcet tones.

Cracked Pepper

Vignette

"Hey!" "Don't put that all over my plate," cried Jeb.

Too late! His mother had already served the steak and without thinking had smothered it in sauce with pepper on top. Well, it could have been worse. It could have been salt that she picked up because she had been distracted while she was serving the meal that night. She had not meant to be so heavy handed but because the snake was lingering near the back door she could not concentrate enough to get things right so Jeb would just have to scrape it off until he got it to his taste. Maybe things would be different if that snake catcher had not just called to say he couldn't come for another hour or two.

Really!!

Understanding

Circle **Yes** or **No** to answer the question.

a. The first sentence in Birdsong, Sweet! is
- ◯ a question
- ◯ a command
- ◯ a statement
- ◯ an exclamation

b. The word closest in meaning to 'vignette' is
- ◯ an essay
- ◯ an article
- ◯ a picture
- ◯ a cameo

c. Cracked Pepper would be
- ◯ bitter
- ◯ sweet
- ◯ hot
- ◯ cold

d. The words closest in meaning to 'distracted'
- ◯ taken aback
- ◯ misunderstood
- ◯ not looking
- ◯ paying attention

Interpreting

Write a question for each of these answers.

a. It could have been salt that mum picked up. ____________________

b. Because the snake was lingering near the back door. ____________________

c. Their crisp, clean call. ____________________

d. Listen. Just listen. ____________________

e. Dulcet Tones. A Disastrous Night. ____________________

Grammar

Adverbs of Place – Where Words – Inside, Outside, Above, Below etc.

Underline the adverbial phrase in each sentence and write it on the line.

a. He placed the book over there. on the table. ____________________

b. We put the bins outside the fence near the road to be emptied. ____________________

c. The new pool sits above ground between the house and shed. ____________________

d. The horse fell into the dam near our house. ____________________

e. The markets will be inside the hall at Smithton if it rains. ____________________

Unit 26

Spelling

Root Word **'hemi'** from the Greek meaning 'half'

Use your dictionary to write the meaning of 'hemisphere'.

Hemisphere ______________________________

Write hemisphere as an **adjective** ______________________________

Word Meanings: Match each word to its meaning.

attribute, compromise, dulcet, distract, lingering, concentrate

a. hanging around ______________ **b.** a quality, property ______________

c. sweet on the ear ______________ **d.** divert attention ______________

e. paying attention ______________ **f.** without favour ______________

Word Building

Use the Prefix – semi – to build words.

trailer, breve, tone, detached, colon, circle

a. ______________

b. ______________

c. ______________

d. ______________

e. ______________

f. ______________

Punctuation

Capital Letters and Full Stops

Re-write each sentence using the correct punctuation.

a. dr and mrs dib are coming to christmas carols in the park

____

b. the new principal is mr abdul and the new teacher will be mrs shahidi

____

c. paul and josie share the same birthday 1 september

____

d. matthew and patrick are brothers and sam and valentina are their brother and sister

____

Credit Card

1. List two things you can buy with an EFTPOS card.

____

2.

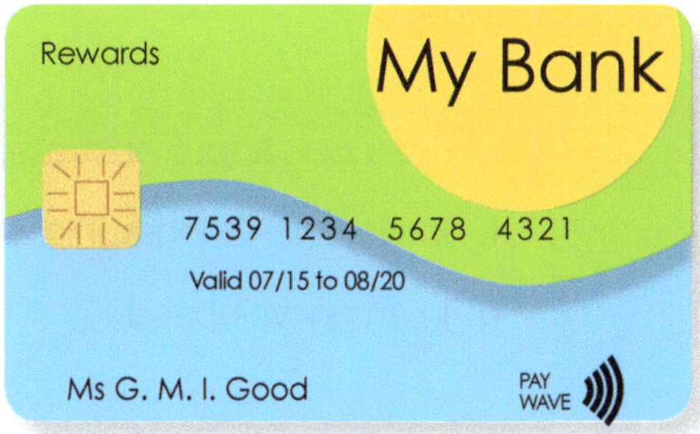

a. What is the EFTPOS card number?

____

b. Which bank issued the card?

____

c. Whose name appears on the card?

____

d. What does the))) symbol mean?

____

e. When does this card expire? ______________

Money

1. Colour the items that attract a GST.

a.

b.

c.

d.

e.

f.

g.

2. Look at each discount and find the new price for the item.

a.

20% off

New price ______________

b.

25% off

New price ______________

c.

40% off

New price ______________

d.

50% off

New price ______________

What is a desert? Many people think of a desert as kilometres and kilometres of sand. But they are not all like that. Some are rocky and have plants or shrubs growing on them. They can be hot and dry as well as icy and cold like those in the Antarctic or the North Pole. This report is about the hot and dry desert.

The hot and dry deserts all share a common feature: they do not get much rain or precipitation. Some might be lucky to receive 1mm of rain in a year. This makes the soil so dry and any rain that does fall just runs off the surface or it evaporates before it hits the ground.

Because the desert is so dry and with a very high humidity and no vegetation to keep the ground moist, the heat is soon lost when night falls. Then it becomes very cold overnight. The temperature range in some deserts can be above 400 during the day to below 00 during the night.

The World's largest hot, dry desert is the Sahara Desert. The Sahara is a sandy desert with large dunes in Northern Africa. Other major World deserts are the Arabian Desert in The Middle East, the Gobi Desert in Northern China and Mongolia and the Kalahari Desert in Africa.

Of course there is the Simpson Desert in Australia with hot, dry days and cold nights. This area, in Central Australia, can catch unsuspecting travellers unprepared for the extreme heat of day or the rapid drop in overnight temperature.

Understanding

Circle **Yes** or **No** to answer each statement.

a. All deserts are the same.	**Yes**	**No**	**b.** There are deserts in Australia.	**Yes**	**No**
c. It is hot and dry in all deserts.	**Yes**	**No**	**d.** Rain soaks into desert soils.	**Yes**	**No**
e. The largest desert is in Africa.	**Yes**	**No**	**f.** One desert is in two countries.	**Yes**	**No**
g. People can die in deserts.	**Yes**	**No**	**h.** Deserts are hot in day and cold at night.	**Yes**	**No**

Interpreting

Where might you find this text? Tick as many as you wish.

a. In a library. ☐	**b.** In a geography book. ☐	**c.** In a book about Australia. ☐
d. In a magazine. ☐	**e.** On a wall chart. ☐	**f.** In National Geographic. ☐
g. On the Internet. ☐	**h.** In a travel guide. ☐	**i.** In an encyclopaedia. ☐

Grammar

Descriptive Adjectives

Underline the descriptive adjectives in each sentence.

a. Icy, cold deserts can be found in Antarctica but the Gobi Desert is a hot, dry desert.

b. Rocky deserts can have large plants growing in them or they can be enormous areas of hot, dry land.

c. The Kalahari Desert in Africa and the Simpson Desert in Australia have hot, dry days and cold nights.

d. Extreme heat and freezing cold temperatures are the well-known features of most World deserts.

e. Dry soil, high humidity and very little precipitation make deserts harsh and dangerous places.

Unit 27

Spelling

Homophones – whether, weather, wether

Write the meaning of each word and then use it in a sentence.

a. whether ______________________________

b. weather ______________________________

c. wether ______________________________

Syllabification: Write each word in syllables.

a. evaporation ____________ **b.** vegetation ____________

c. precipitation ____________ **d.** temperature ____________

e. kilometre ____________

f. Arabian ____________

g. Kalahari ____________

h. Mongolia ____________

Word Building

Add Prefix 'sub' to form new words.

way, ject, merge, lime, mariner, scription, sequent, terranean, divide

a. ____________

b. ____________

c. ____________

d. ____________

e. ____________

f. ____________

g. ____________

h. ____________

i. ____________

Punctuation

Question Mark or Exclamation Mark

Mark the correct punctuation on the following.

a. Stop **b.** Is it dry **c.** Can you swim **d.** Run Tom **e.** Are you wet he asked

Circles

1. Measure the radius of each circle.

a.  r = ________mm

b. 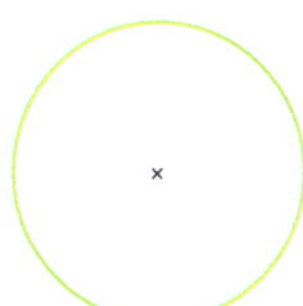 r = ________mm

c. 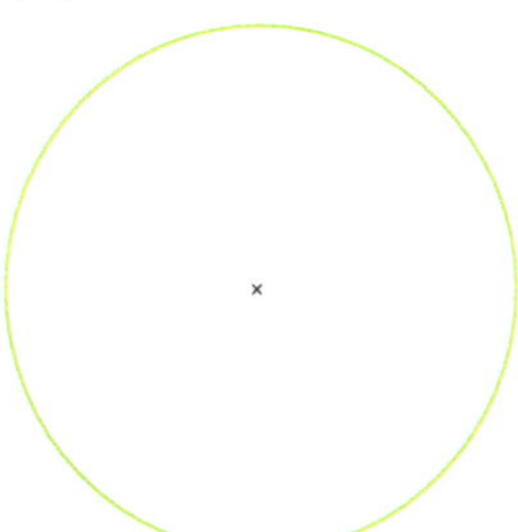 r = ________ mm

2. Measure the diameter of each circle.

a. d = ________mm

b. 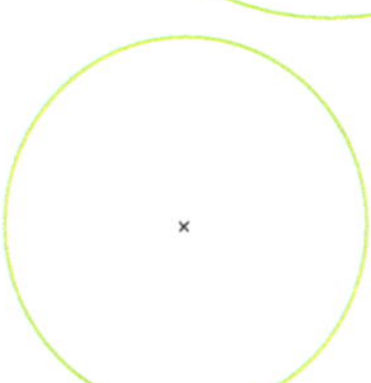 d = ________mm

c. d = ________mm

3D Objects

Name the 3D objects drawn from various viewpoints and projections.

1. 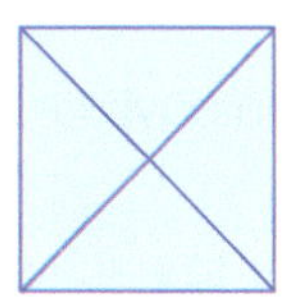 ____________

2. 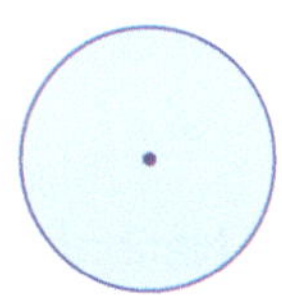 ____________

3. 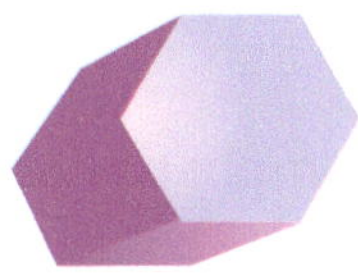 ____________

4. 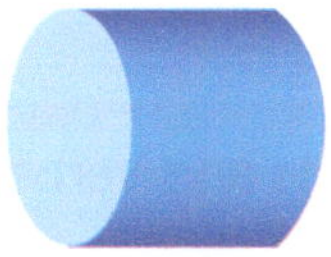 ____________

5. 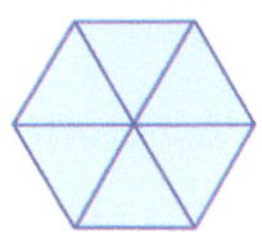 ____________

6. 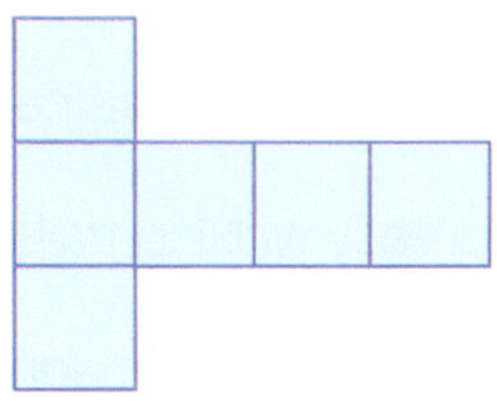 ____________

Uluru and the Olgas

Factual Description

Within the heart of Australia's Red Centre lie Uluru and the Olgas, in Uluru-Kata-Tjuta National Park. The Olgas are dome-like shaped rocks believed to have formed around the same time as Ayres Rock (Uluru). Now there are 36 formations that make up the Olgas, but thousands of years ago it is thought to have been just one rock formation like Uluru.

The Olgas are 35kms west of Uluru and the highest point is Mount Olga which rises 546m above the ground. This is 200m higher than Ayres Rock and has a circumference of 22kms while Ayres Rock is only 10km. The big difference between the two sites is, at the Olgas it is possible to walk through valleys and crevices but it is not possible to do so at Uluru. One well known place for tourists to visit is the Valley of the Winds. The views there are spectacular and walking tracks provide opportunities for everyone to experience great sights and sounds for themselves. These tracks range in distance from just under one kilometre to seven kilometres.

To enjoy the beauty of this place it is advisable to begin exploring early in the day, before the sun becomes too hot and unbearable. Of course, not everyone who visits this marvellous site can undertake a long distance walk or even withstand the heat. However, the Kata-Tjuta Dune is within easy walking distance of the car park and allows a wonderful viewpoint from there.

Just like Uluru, the Olgas or Kata-Tjuta (meaning many heads) has been home to the Anangu people for thousands of years. At night, this local tribe often perform ceremonies and rituals on their land, as they have done down through the centuries to this present day.

Understanding

Tick the box if the information is in the text.

a. Uluru is the Aboriginal name for Ayres Rock. ☐

b. Kata-Tjuta means many heads. ☐

c. Once the Olgas were a one rock formation. ☐

d. It is possible to walk through the Olgas. ☐

e. The Valley of the Winds is at Uluru. ☐

f. Anangu is the local Aboriginal Tribe at Uluru. ☐

g. Domes in the Olgas are taller than Uluru. ☐

h. Walking tracks at the Olgas are kilometres in length. ☐

i. It is too hot to walk in the Olgas in daytime. ☐

j. Everyone can walk around the Olgas. ☐

Interpreting

Write an answer to each question.

a. Why is it best to walk around the Olgas? ______________________________

b. How long have people lived in this National Park? ______________________________

c. What are Uluru and the Olgas? ______________________________

d. Can you name a ceremony that might be held there? ______________________________

e. What would be the closest city or town to Uluru and the Olgas? ______________________________

Grammar

Sentence **Subjects and Verbs** (Predicate)

Underline the verb and write the subject in each sentence on the line.

a. Uluru-Kata-Tjuta National Park is in the Northern Territory of Australia. ______________________________

b. The local tribe perform ceremonies and rituals on their land. ______________________________

c. The Olgas and Uluru formed around the same time. ______________________________

d. The Valley of the Winds has easy walking trails for tourists to enjoy. ______________________________

e. Disabled or elderly visitors can still enjoy magnificent views. ______________________________

Spelling — Unit 28 — Word Building

Homophones – to, two, too Use the homophone correctly in each sentence.

a. We went _____ the beach with the _____ boys from next door.

b. They were _____ tired _____ care about eating dinner at _____ a.m.

c. When the _____ books arrive will you call the _____ people who are waiting _____ collect them.

d. At _____ p.m. the _____ races began before there was _____ much rain on the course.

Proof Reading: Re-write each sentence using **correct spelling**.

a. No dout he nose the right way too swim. _____

b. There books will be redy wen he is. _____

c. Them cows are two sick to moov. _____

d. Sudenly the grond opend up. _____

Gender - Masculine or Feminine, Common or Neuter. Write **M** or **F**, **C** or **N** in each box to identify the gender of each word.

a. colt ☐ **b.** bull ☐ **c.** drake ☐

d. heroine ☐ **e.** baby ☐

f. friend ☐ **g.** mare ☐ **h.** cow ☐

i. parent ☐ **j.** chair ☐

Punctuation

Abbreviations and Titles

Write abbreviations for

a. Justice of the Peace _____ **b.** Master of Ceremonies _____ **c.** south south west _____

Re-write this sentence using correct punctuation.

d. mr and mrs fahmi went to see madam butterfly at the sydney opera house.

_____

Faces and Nets

1. Match each 3D object to its net.

a.

e.
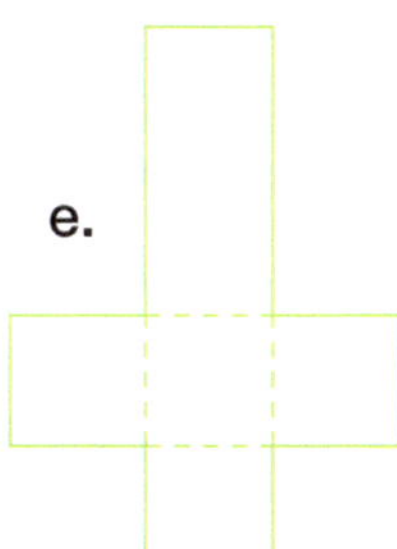

f.
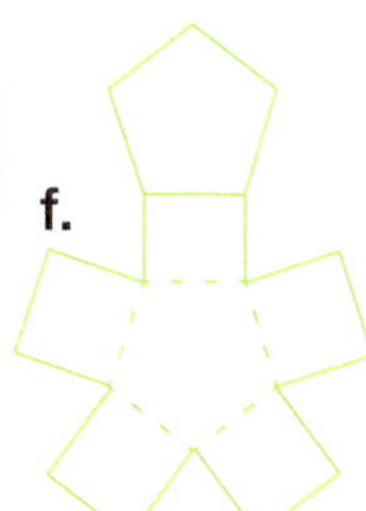

b.
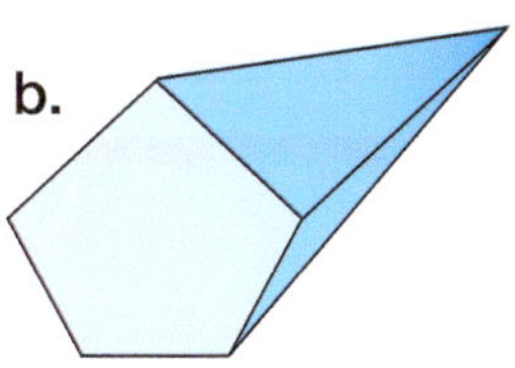

c.
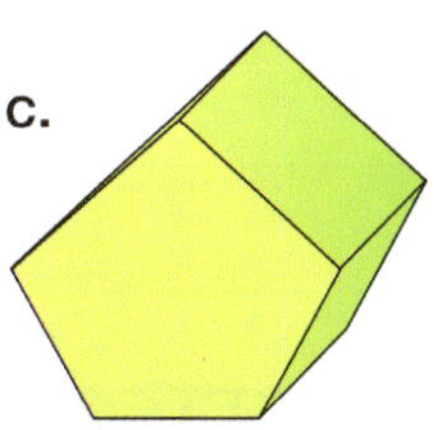

g.

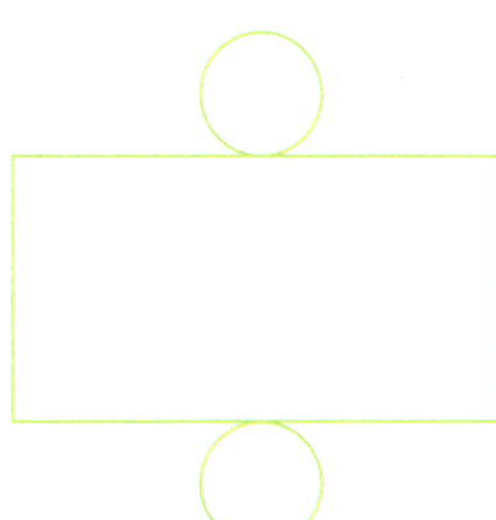

d.
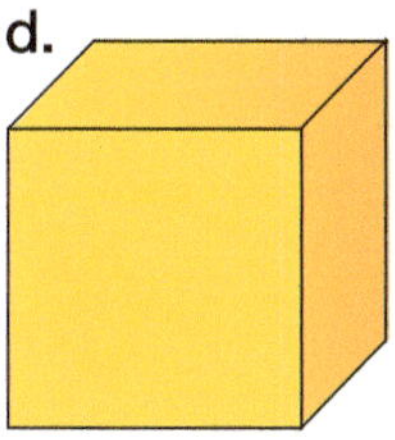

h.

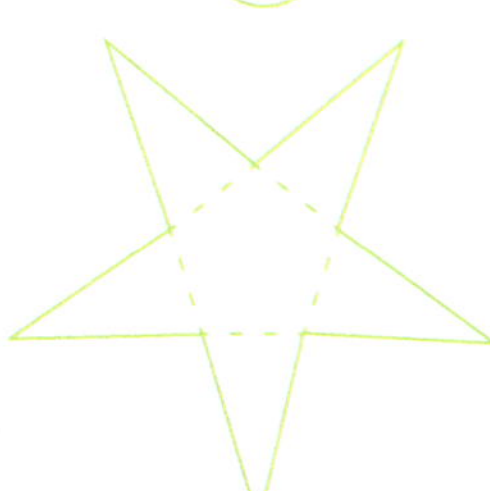

Location

1. Identify the position of objects on the grid. Draw the shape alongside the co-ordinates.

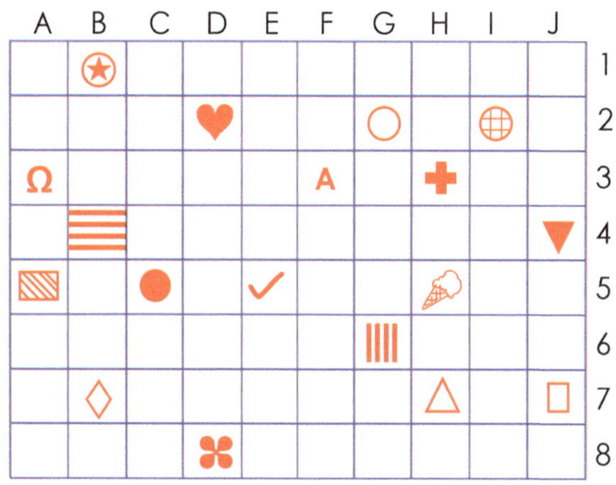

a. G6 _____ **b.** A3 _____ **c.** B1 _____

d. G2 _____ **e.** H7 _____ **f.** H3 _____

g. D8 _____ **h.** C5 _____ **i.** I2 _____

j. H5 _____ **k.** B4 _____ **l.** J7 _____

m. F3 _____ **n.** A6 _____ **o.** D2 _____

p. B7 _____ **q.** J4 _____ **r.** E5 _____

Holiday Fun

Narrative/Recount

At last! School holidays are nearly here. We'll be ready to take off then on our annual camping holiday. Our family has a permanent booking at the same ground each year. As a matter of fact they've been going to the same camping ground in Tuncurry for the past twenty years.

As the time draws closer, excitement rises, because we know the same group of 'camping' buddies will be ready for a fun time together. There'll all be there looking forward to another round of fishing fun, on the shimmering sands, with daily delights like playing games and talking together, always assured of catching up on a year gone by and making grand plans for the one to come. All the families are the best of friends so most activities are interwoven for the whole holiday. We might have a picnic lunch or a barbeque tea in the late afternoon when everyone's finished playing, swimming or fishing.

What better way to spend a six week holiday; fishing, boating, swimming, walking or just lazing around reading or talking and catching up on the past year? Ah! Familiar delight: another year in perspective. It's races and cricket when it isn't too hot. After lunch we might find time to walk into town to buy glow sticks and other gear for the New Year's Eve party.

The big attraction on New Year's Eve is the fireworks as they light up the sky early in the evening and again at midnight. Most of the time we just play on the sandy shore waiting for a fantastic fireworks display to herald in the change of year. Then we have a short walk back to camp. Needless to say we are very tired to start off the New Year, which can be rather hot, so we might find the energy for a morning dip.

Can you think of a better way to say "hello" to a New Year while celebrating with old friends?

Understanding

Shade the bubble for the best answer.

a. The holidays are long. ☐

b. The kids can walk into town from their campsite. ☐

c. The fireworks are a highlight of these holidays. ☐

d. Few people go camping in the school holidays. ☐

e. There is a barbeque for lunch and a picnic for tea. ☐

Interpreting

Write the meaning of:

a. annual ________ **b.** permanent ________

c. herald in ________ **d.** gear ________

e. attraction ________ **f.** needless to say ________

g. perspective ________ **h.** assured ________

i. celebrate ________ **j.** familiar ________

Grammar

Write each contracted word in full.

a. we're ________ **b.** they're ________ **c.** they'll ________

d. we'll ________ **e.** it's ________ **f.** isn't ________

g. there'll ________ **h.** who'll ________ **i.** we've ________

j. shan't ________ **k.** would've ________ **l.** must've ________

Word Building

The Suffix – ness – meaning a state of being. Add the suffix 'ness' and write a new word.

a. sick ________ **b.** bright ________ **c.** foolish ________

d. weak ________ **e.** thick ________ **f.** aware ________

g. great ________ **h.** expensive ________ **i.** comfortable ________

Revision Exercises — Unit 30

Spelling Rule: Change 'y' to 'I' to add Suffix'ness' to a word. Add the suffix 'ness' and write a new word.

a. happy ______________________ **b.** lazy ______________________ **c.** merry ______________________

d. crazy ______________________ **e.** scary ______________________ **f.** hungry ______________________

g. greedy ______________________ **h.** ready ______________________ **i.** lonely ______________________

Alphabetical Order: Occupations Write these words in correct alphabetical order.

author navigator conductor sculptor governor tailor sailor doctor inspector

a. ______________________ **b.** ______________________ **c.** ______________________

d. ______________________ **e.** ______________________ **f.** ______________________

g. ______________________ **h.** ______________________ **i.** ______________________

Punctuation: Broken Speech and **Inverted Commas**

Mark the inverted commas and other punctuation marks correctly in each sentence.

a. I will be ready by two oclock jane but i cant get a bus until two thirty

b. why is the game so early cried dad i wont be ready at that time

c. does he know where to put the new furniture when it is delivered mum asked or will it be left outside

Location

Use the map of Samson to answer each question.

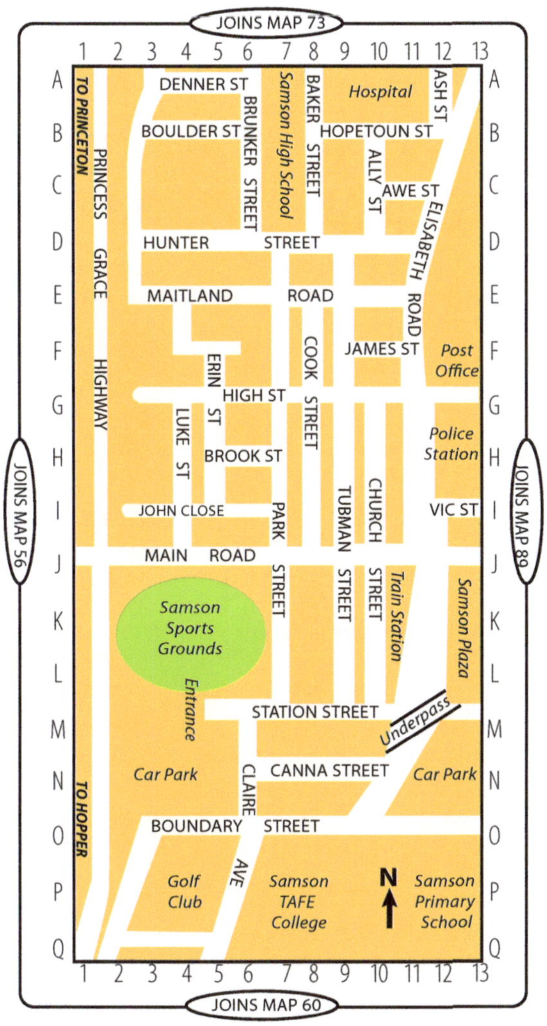

1. What is found at K4? ______________________

2. What landmark is found at F12? ______________________

3. What type of sporting ground is found south of the Sports Ground? ______________________

4. Give the co-ordinates for the primary school. ______________________

5. What is found at M10? ______________________

6. In what direction does Cook St run? ______________________

7. In what direction is the Police Station from the train station? ______________________

8. Give the co-ordinates for the intersection of Main Road and Princess Grace Highway. ______________________

9. What is north-east of the high school? ______________________

10. In which direction does Main Road run? ______________________

11. In which direction is Princeton? ______________________

12. What can be found at N12? ______________________

Answers

Unit 1	**Understanding: a.** The Annual Surf Spectacular. **b.** From early morning until they started to feel hungry. **c.** School **d.** The boys got hungry. **e.** The ocean. **f.** At the Annual Surfing Competition. **Interpreting:** circle **a.**T **b.**F **c.**T **d.**F **e.**T **f.**T **Grammar: a.** long, summer school holidays **b.** Annual Surf Spectacular **c.** cantankerous **d.**big day and junior competition **e.** early morning **f.** past years **Word Building: a.** cried, crying **b.**competed, competing **c.**returned, returning **Spelling: a.** hurried **b.** tried **c.** terrified **d.** studied **Syllabification: a.** spec/ tac/ u/ lar **b.** squealed **c.** gua/ ran/ tee **d.** treach/ er/ ous **e.** can/ tank/ er/ ous **f.** ex/ pec/ ta/ tions **Punctuation: a.** Phil and John went to the Sunday matinee. **b.** The boys joined the Bears Football Team together. **c.** In February, the Prime Minister, Mrs Albright, visited our school. **Place Value: 1. a.** 34 155 **b.** 13 563 **c.** 70 673 **2.a.** thousands **b.** hundreds **c.** thousands **3.a.** 64 276 **b.** 72 942 **c.** 38 751 **Addition:1.a.** 107 **b.**108 **c.**189 **d.** 338 **2.a.** 8 665 **b.** 7 695 **c.** 6 692 **d.** 8 443
Unit 2	**Understanding:** Tick b, d, e, f, g, i, j. **Interpreting:a.** vegetation **b.** average **c.** tropical **d.** resembling **e.** plentiful **f.** canopy **Grammar:a.** enormous **b.** average **c.** hot, humid **d.** many **e.** Information **f.** more dangerous **Word Building: a.** spread **b.** thread **c.**dread **a.** spend **b.** trend **c.** blend **Spelling: a.** reign **b.** rain **c.**rein **Syllabification: a.** trop/i/cal **b.** en/or/mous **c.** can/o/pies **d.** dif/fer/ent **e.** rain/for/est **f.** plen/ti/ful **Punctuation: a.** The Junior Red Cross **b.** Her Majesty, Queen Elizabeth **c.** The Royal Australian Air Force **d.**The honourable, Judge John Dew. **Subtraction: 1.a.** 413 **b.** 555 **c.** 434 **d.** 222 **2.a.** 3 227 **b.** 5 725 **c.** 5 253 **d.** 2 636 **Multiplication: 1.** Parent to check. Answers = **a.** 2 464 **b.** 9 366 **c.** 4 888 **2.**180, 810, 450, 2 700, 900, 630, 540, 90
Unit 3	**Understanding:** Shade **a.** 3 **b.** 1 **c.** 4 **d.** 1 **Interpreting: a.** Ireland **b.** From Southhampton to New York **c.** 3 days **d.** An iceberg cut a hole in its side **e.**There were not enough life boats for everyone on board. **Grammar: a.** so **b.** but **a.** and **Word Bullding: a.** clear **b.**shear **c.**spear **d.**smear **Spelling: a.** wrong **b.** wreck **c.** write **d.** wrinkle **e.** wrap **f.** writhe **g.** wrestle **h.** wrath **i.** wring **Syllabification:a.** be/ginn/ing **b.** ac/com/mo/dat/ing **c.** un/sink/a/ble **d.** sub/merged **e.** col/lid/ed **f.** dis/cov/ered **Punctuation: a.** ? **b.** ! **c.** ? **d.** ! **e.** ? **f.** ! **g.** ? **h.** ! **i.** ? **Factors and Multiples: 1. a.** 1, 12, 2, 6, 3, 4, **b.** 1, 15, 3, 5 **c.** 1, 20, 2, 10, 4, 5 **d.** 1, 39, 3, 13 **2.a.** T **b.** T **c.** T **d.** F **3a.** 27, 81, 18 **b.** 36, 42 **Division:1. a.** 10 **b.** 9 **c.** 8 **d.** 8 **2a.** 28 ÷ 4 = 7 **b.** 39 ÷ 3 = 13 **c.** 24 ÷ 6 = 4
Unit 4	**Understanding:** Tick All. **Interpreting: a.** These are called 'southerly busters'. **b.** Isolation occurs due to properties being cut off by floods. **c.** You would be in the northern part of Australia. **d.** December, January and February **e.** Parent. **Grammar: a.** Australia high and low pressure systems weather patterns. **b.** Southern Ocean and Great Australian Bight; summer. **c.** Cyclone Mary, Cyclone Nina. **d.** "Freemantle Doctor", Perth cool change, hot, summer day. **e.** Australia, summer rains, minor flooding, east coast. **Word Building: a.** believed **b.** believing **c.** believable **d.** believably **e.** unbelievable **Spelling Rule:a.** factories **b.** properties **c.** histories **d.** studies **e.** babies **f.** curries **g.** hurries **h.** stories **Syllabification: a.** Aus/tra/li/an **b.** pat/terns **c.** south/er/ly **d.** pro/per/ties **e.** al/pha/bet **f.** sea/son/al. **Punctuation: a.** John and Mary are going to Port Douglas for their holidays. **b.** The Australian War Memorial is in Canberra. **c.** Sydney, Brisbane and Hobart are all on the east coast of Australia. **Decimal Fractions:1.a.** 0.6 **b.** 0.3 **c.** 0.7 **2.a.** 0.5 **b.** 0.9 **c.** 0.3 **d.** 2/10 or 1/5 **e.** 7/10 **f.** 0.25 **g.** 0.8 **h.** 6/10 or 3/5 **3a.** parent **Percentages: 1a.** 36% **b.** 67% **2.a.** 74% **b.** 85% **c.** 32% **d.** 68% **3a.** 0.75, 75% **b.** 4/10 or 2/5, 40% **c.** 32/100, 0.32 **d.** 0.9, 90% **e.** 25/100 or ¼ , 25%
Unit 5	**Understanding:** Shade **1a.** 3 **b.** 2 **c.** 3 **d.** 3 **Interpreting:a.** No **b.** Yes **c.** Yes **d.** Yes **e.** Yes **Grammar: a.** allow, extend **b.** secure, attach **Word Building: a.** paw **b.** pour **c.** poor, pour. **Spelling: a.** piece, tail, kite **b.** need, duct, newspaper **c.** There, many, loose **d.** ribbon, ninety, length. **AO:** kill, kite, piece, plastic, rhyme, ribbon, scissors, string, tamper, tape. **Punctuation: a.** it is **b.** they are **c.** you will **d.** cannot **e.** there is **f.** would not **g.** shall not **h.** we are **Rounding Off: 1. a.** 80 **b.** 100 **c.** 50 **d.** 80 **e.** 30 **f.** 40 **g.** 50 **h.** 20 **i.** 90 **2a.** \$2.35 **b.** \$5.00 **c.** \$10.45 **d.** \$7.20 **e.** \$12.55 **f.** \$8.80 **3a.** 8 000 **b.** 5 000 **c.** 3 000 **d.** 4 000 **e.** 4 000 **f.** 4 000 **Patterns:1a.** Divide by 5 **b.** double each number **c.** multiply by ten **d.** multiply by 3. **2a.** 0.6 **b.** 4/10 **c.** 3/8 **d.** 6.0 **e.** 5/6
Unit 6	**Understanding:** Parent to check poetry. Shade **a.** 2 **b.** 4 **c.** 3 **d.** 4 **Interpreting:a.** yes **b.** no **c.** yes **d.** yes **e.** yes **Grammar:a.** quickly, because **b.** underneath **c.** tomorrow, beside. **Word Building:a.** somewhere **b.** something **c.** someone **d.** somebody **e.** someday **f.** sometimes **Spelling Rule: a.** donkeys **b.** monkeys **c.** valleys **d.** journeys **e.** trolleys **f.** turkeys **Syllabification:a.** Hai/ku **b.** hung/ry **c.** whimp/er **d.** ex/am/ples **e.** for/ev/er **f.** but/cher **Punctuation: a.** they'll **b.** he's **c.** haven't **d.** I'm **e.** you've **f.** can't **g.** should've **h.** would've **i.** I'd **j.** it's **Length: 1 a.** 0.3m **b.** 0.258m **2a.** 11cm **b.** 11cm **3a.** cm **b.** mm **c.** m **d.** mm **e.** m **Area: 1a.** 12cm² **b.**11cm² **2a.** 600 cm² **b.** 375cm² **c.** 3.75m² **d.**150mm²

Answers

Unit 7	**Understanding:** Tick a,b,c,d,e,f **Interpreting:a.** You might find snakes, insects, frogs, birds, lizards, iguanas, large boas, jaguars, monkeys, bats and large birds of prey in the rainforest. **b.**The large boa squeezes its victim to death. **c.**There could be iguanas in the rainforest. **d.** Bats and monkeys swing and hang upside down in the trees. **e.** Small shrubs grow up to 5 metres and trees grow to great heights. **Grammar:a.** "Hurry up!" before it is dark. **b.**The computer didn't work after we used it. **c.** Now is the time if you can show me how. **d.** I can bake the cake when the oven is hot. **e.** She missed the first lesson because the bus was late. **Word Building:a.** artist **b.** florist **c.** organist **d.** cyclist **Spelling Rule: a.** careful **b.** doubtful **c.** powerful **d.** successful **e.** playful **f.** peaceful **Dictionary Use: a.** within either of the two parallels of latitude on the globe **b.** to pierce into, go through **c.** very thick **d.** a particular type or group with the same characteristics **e.** an immeasurable number **f.** large birds hunting for food **Punctuation: a.** Because of the rain, the class was unhappy **b.** When the sun came out, we were happy **c.** Tom had a red, green, gold and yellow pencil. **d.** After dark, we will look at the moon. **e.** Players four, five, six, nine and ten are here. **f.** Before the sun rises, we will go fishing. **Capacity:1a.** 3 500 mL **b.** 1 500 mL **c.** 1 000 mL **d.** 2 250 mL **e.** 2 500 mL **f.** 5 250 mL **2a.** 700 mL **b.** 500 mL **c.** 850 mL **3a.** 0.375 **b.** 0.6 **c.** 0.4 **d.** 0.75 **e.** 0.25 **f.** 0.35 **Volume:1a.**12 **b.**10 **2a.**32 cm^2 **b.**54 cm^2
Unit 8	**Understanding:** Shade **a.** 3 **b.** 2 **c.** 3 **d.** 3 **Interpreting:** Tick a, b, c, d, e, f **Grammar:a.** yours **b.** you, me **c.** I, him **d.** Your, ours Underline **a.** I, our **b.** we, my **c.** you, his **d.** it, they, their **Word Building: a.** doctor or nurse **b.** tailor **c.** author **d.** sculptor **e.** navigator **Spelling:a.** men **b.** teeth **c.** feet **d.** women **e.** mice **f.** geese **g.** lice **h.** children **Dictionary Use: a.** narrow beams of light **b.** overspread with clouds **c.** to uncover or display **d.** skin cancer **AO:** exposure, melanoma, overcast, rays **Punctuation:a.** Without a doubt **b.** I think **c.** we should do it. **Angles: 1a.** obtuse **b.** reflex **c.** right **d.** acute **2a.** right angle **b.** straight angle **c.** obtuse angle **2D Shapes:1a.** square **b.** rectangle **c.** pentagon **d.** hexagon **e.** triangle **2a.** 4 diagonals **b.** 6 diagonals
Unit 9	**Understanding:** Parent: a.b.c.d. Circle e.Y **Interpreting: a.** There are two fish dishes on the menu. **b.** Sausages and potatoes **c.** The cheap days for children to eat are Monday and Tuesday. **d.** Children under 2 do not eat very much. **e.** $22 **Grammar:** Cross **a.** who **b.** that **c.** who **d.** whom **e.** that **f.** which **g.** which **h.** which **Word Building: a.** improves **b.** improved **c.** improving **d.** improvement **a.** invests **b.** invested **c.** investing **d.** investment **Spelling: a.** Prime **b.** Primary **c.** primer **d.** prime primitive **Syllabification: a.** fab/u/lous **b.** en/trées **c.** spa/ghet/ti **d.** ba/na/na **e..** fla/vour/ing **f.** des/sert **Punctuation:** "Do not stand on the grass!" cried Jack. **Nets: 1.** Cylinder **2.** Square pyramid **c.** cube **d.** hexagonal pyramid **Mass: 1a.** 42kg **b.** 38kg **c.** 43kg **d.** 27kg **2a.** 0.835kg **b.**1.25g **c.** 0.165g **d.** 2kg **e.** 1.5kg **f.** 2.235kg
Unit 10	**Understanding:a.** It is too dangerous to climb the rock and it is a sacred site. **b.** Uluru is in the Northern Territory of Australia. **c.** geological phenomenon **d.** Uluru and Ayres Rock **e.** The weather and the different times of day causes changes to the rock. **Interpreting:** Shade **a.** 1 **b.**1 **c.**4 **d.** 4 **Grammar:** Underline during late afternoon **b.** by bus, car or plane **c.** at one time of day **d.** over its sides **e.** in the mid-1980s **f.** inside the caves **Word Building:** Parent check **Spelling: a.** almost **b.** always **c.** although **d.** already **e.** also **f.** altogether **AO:** crevices, geology, monolith, nomenclature, palpable, spectrum **Punctuation: a.** Uluru, Ayres Rock **b.** Northern Territory **c.** The Olgas, Kata-Tjuta **24 Hour Time: 1a.**16:45 **b.** 13:40 **c.**18:55 **2a.**18:30 **b.** 08:45 **3.a.**  **b.**  **c.**  **Temperature: 1a.b.c.d.** parent **2a.**100°C b.42°C 3a. 50°C b. 26°C c. 60°C
Unit 11	**Understanding:** Tick a.b.c.g,h **Interpreting: a.** demise **b.** enthusiastic **c.** eucalypt **d.** ingest **e.** dedicated **f.** extinct **Grammar: a.** good, better, best **b.** bad, worse, worst **c.** good, better, best **Word Building:** parent to check **Spelling:** Circle **a.** won, aminals – write: one, animals **b.** circle: kowalas, fir, clause, larje write: koalas, fur, claws, large **c.** circle: loging, distroing, there, habbitats. write: logging, destroying, their, habitats **d.** circle: entusiasts, worriers. write: enthusiasts, warriors Missing letters: **a.** e,u,a,y **b.** o,o,u,e **c.** a,e,a **d.** e,i,u **e.** o,o,u,i,i,e **f.** a,a,i **Punctuation: a.** Thumb's **b.** Smith's **c.** children's **d.** various species' **e.** lady's **f.** Joneses' **Graphs: 1.** 80 **2.** Monday **3.** 5 **4.** Monday **Location: 1.** B10 **2.** C4 **3.** D9 **4.** E2 **5.** B6 **6.** G10 **7.** A2 **8.** H5 **9.** H3 **10.** C8
Unit 12	**Understanding:** Circle: Yes **b.** Yes **c.** No **d.** Yes **e.** Yes **Interpreting: a.** Whether children should work for pocket money? **b.** If pocket money should be earned, at what age and what should a child do with their pocket money. **c.** Nine year olds can review the tasks and the amount to be given to them. **d.** It is important for a teenager to work out how much to spend and how much to save. **e.** discuss **Grammar: a.** under the tree **b.** across the road **c.** near the front gate **d.** between the fence **Word Building: a.b.c.d.** Parent **Spelling: a.** centipede **b.** biped **c.** pedicure **d.** pedestrian **e.** pedal **Syllabification:a.** con/ten/tious **b.** gra/tu/i/tous **c.** per/for/mance **d.** ne/go/ti/a/ted **e.** re/viewed **f.** in/di/vid/u/al **Punctuation:** they're, their **b.** there, their **c.** there, they're, their **d.** your, you, your **e.** you're, you **Problems: 1.** 99÷3=33 each **2.**3 **3.**48 **4.**2 505kms **Probabilities: 1a.**0 **b.** parent **c.**0.5 **d.**parent **e.**1 **f.**0.5 **2a.**0.25 **b.**0.25 **c.**0.25 **d.**0.25
Unit 13	**Understanding: a.**A **b.**D **c.**A **d.**D **e.**B **f.**B **g.**A **h.**B **Interpreting: a.**4 **b.**Signal the driver to stop for you. **c.**You could catch the wrong bus or you could miss the bus you want to catch.**d.**The buses are going to different suburbs and important places in a city. **e.** Because this is just a sample of an area where buses stop. **Grammar:a.** with, outside **b.** around, quietly **c.** with, indoors **d.** alone **e.** between **Word Building:a.** unhappy **b.** unlikely **c.** unsuitable **d.** unopened **e.** impure **f.** impatient **g.** immovable **h.** impolite **Spelling:** minute= small amount, part of an hour, sow = a female pig, to plant crops etc. **Proof Reading:a.** board, correct **b.** must, signal **c.** Central Railway **d.** East Gardens, Airport **Punctuation: a.** they're **b.** we've **c.** you're **d.** it's **e.** they're **f.** we'll **Transformation: 1.** Parent **2** .Parent **Shopping:1.**$20.89 **2.**$60 **3.**$80 **4.**34 **5.**240

Answers

Unit 14	**Understanding:** Shade: **a.**3 **b.**4 **c.**3 **d.**1 **Interpreting: a.**Clock-wise **b.**Both are very strong and dangerous. **c.**The wind and the rotation of the Earth. **d.** Underwater eruptions cause tsunamis. **e.** rips or undertows **Grammar: a.** the water in the ocean, dangerous rips **b.** waves of different sizes and strength **c.** waves, energy **d.** waves, great distances **e.** swells, the waves and ocean **f.** swells, top of crests, bottom **Word Building:** parent check **Spelling:a.** solid wood **b.** with no interest **c.** a certificate giving formal permission **d.** granting permission to do **e.** writing materials **f.** being parked or at a standstill **g.** one who depends on another **h.** depending on something else **f.** a repeated performance **g.** to perform or repeat activity to acquire a skill **Syllabification: a.** ro/ta/tion **b.** grav/i/ta/tion/al **c.** fric/tion **d.**dev/as/ta/ting **e.** hem/i/sphere **f.** dif/fer/ence **Punctuation: a.** ante-meridian **b.** post-meridian **c.** Eastern Standard Time **d.** Greenwich Mean Time **e.** Australian Eastern Daylight Time **Tessellation: 1.** Colour a,c,d,e,g,i,j,l **2a.**draw a-f, b-e, c-h, d-g **Polygons: 1a.** square **b.** trapezium **c.** pentagon **d.** rectangle **2a.**3 **b.**2 **c.**2 **d.**5
Unit 15	**Understanding: a.**T **b.**T **c.**T **d.**F **e.**T **f.**T **g.**F **h.**T **i.**T **j.**F **Interpreting: a.** Special and welcome **b.** She feels important, happy and glad to see her. **c.** At her next visit. **d.** Bec feels very pleased to have made a present and she is excited about giving it to Baba. **e.** It is not the gift that matters but the thought of giving a gift that counts. **Grammar: a.** dangerous **b.** famous **c.** beautiful **d.** icy **e.** dreadful **f.** selfish **g.** delightful **h.** easy **j.** thickish **Word Building:** parent check **Spelling:** Parent check **Proof Reading: a.**i,r,a,y **b.** e,e **c.** p,l,e,d **d.** e,m,e,m,e,w,r **Punctuation: a.** Wow! **b.** Stop! **c.** Quick march! **Equivalent Fractions: 1.**3/10 **2.**7/8 **3.**1/5, 3/10, 1/2, 3/5, 7/10, 4/5 **4a.**4/8 **b.**1/5 **c.**2/4 **d.**2/12 **5a.**3/4 **b.**5/6 **c.** 8/10 **Decimals: 1.** In order on line – 0.3, 0.4, 0.5, 0.7, 0.8, 0.9, 1.1, 1.2, 1.6, 1.9 **2a.**0.5 **b.**2.3 **c.**1.7 **d.**0.75 **e.**1.0 **f.**1.0 **3a.** 0.3, 0.5 **4a.** 3.2 **b.**2.8
Unit 16	**Understanding:** Shade: **a.**3 **b.**4 **c.**2 **d.**4 **Interpreting: a.** They went in their old beaten up ute. **b.** At school.. **c.** No, because it is the 'latest' calamity to beset them. **d.** As old school friends they often go away for week-ends together. **e.** It could be but most likely no. The review has been written as a sample of how to write a review. **Grammar: a.** red, ballet **b.** new, next **c.** dire, many different **d.** coastal, wonderful **Word Building: a.** hidden **b.** brave **c.** anger **d.** mend **e.** mend **f.** harsh **Spelling: a.** tomatoes **b.** potatoes **c.** heroes **d.** echoes **e.** volcanoes **f.** mosquitoes **g.** avocados **h.** fiascos **i.** photos **j.** Kilos **k.** ratios **l.** videos **Proof Reading: a.** unpredictable, attention **b.** whole, terrain, extraordinary, throughout **c.** experience, wonderful, adventures **Punctuation: a.** "Come quickly!" Dad called. "We have to catch the bus." **b.** "Before long," Josie sighed. "It will be time for bed." **Measuring Angles: 1.** circle b **2a.**75°C **b.** 120°C **3.** Parent **Line Graphs: 1.**40kms **2.**9am **3.**half an hour **4.**4 1/2 hours **5.**10:30am
Unit 17	**Understanding: a.**1770 **b.**1778 **c.**1606 **d.**1793 **e.**1778 **f.**1616 **g.** 26 January **h.**1606 **i.**1790 **j.**1642 **Interpreting: a.**Gadigal **b.** Reigning Monarch **c.**mariner **d.**unknown land **e.**free settlers **f.**Dutch **Grammar: a.** this, that **b.**those, this **c.**these, this **d.**that, that **e.**those, this, this **Word Building: a.** information **b.** encouragement **c.**classification **d.**support **e.**notification **f.**description **Spelling:a.** decide or make a decision **b.** to crush or grind with the teeth **c.** a male pig **d.** to drill, make a hole or lose interest in a thing **e.** boar **f.** choose **g.** chews **h.** bore **Proof Reading: a.** mariners, off **b.** mariners, different, our **c.** Merchant, Indies **d.** Englishman, Lieutenant, East Coast **Punctuation:a.** TD **b.** S **c.** S **d.** O **Location: 1a.** Swim Centre **b.** Barton St **c.** school **d.** Main Street **e.** hospital **f.** supermarket **g.** church **h.** chemist **i.** Joshua Close **j.** Police Station **k.** oval **l.** Opera Hall **Ordering Time: 1a.**1:00pm **b.**7:00am **c.**4:30pm **d.**9:00am **e.**6:30pm **f.**11:00am **g.**8:00am **h.**9:30pm **i.**7:15am **j.**3:00pm **2.** b,i,g,d,f,a,j,c,e,h
Unit 18	**Understanding:** Shade: **a.**3 **b.**4 **c.**1 **d.**2 **Interpreting: a.**There is such a good thing happening in the area like the new shopping centre. **b.**They are so excited about the opportunities now opening up for them to shop. **c.** All day **d.** Good quality shoes, bags and clothes, nice bling, cosmetics, different cuisines **e.**To the cinema. **Grammar: a.** are **b.**is **c.** are **d.** am **e.** are **f.**is Cross out **a.**is **b.**are **c.**is **d.**am, are **Word Building:a.**parent check **Spelling: a.**cricket **b.**bucket **c.**rocket **d.**heckle **e.**cracker **f.** sprocket **Word opposites:** parent check **Syllabification: a.** cin/e/ma **b.**cui/sine **c.**a/vail/a/ble **d.**ex/pe/di/tion **e.**des/tin/a/tion **Punctuation: b.** VC **c.** PO **d.**ACT **e.** NSW **f.** GG **Distance:1a.** NW **b.**Waxton **c.** 8km **d.**C9 **e.**SE **f.**14km **Fractions: 1a.** water sports **b.**50% **c.**25% **d.**netball & cricket **e.**10 **f.**5 **g.**5
Unit 19	**Understanding: a.**Fact **b.**Fact **c.**Fact **d.**Fact **e.**Fact **Interpreting: a.**F **b.**T **c.**T **d.**F **e.**T **f.**T **g.**T **h.**T **i.**F **j.**T **Grammar: a.**audience **b.**swarm **c.**school **d.**fleet **e.**congregation **f.**flock **g.**pack **h.**herd **i.**choir **j.**team **Word Building: a.** critical **b.**criticise **c.**creepy **d.**crumble **e.**crony **f.**crucial **g.**cruise **h.**crusade **Spelling:a.**quarrelled, quarrelling, quarreller **b.**travelled, travelling, traveller **c.**marvelled, marvelling, marveller **d.**propelled, propelling, propeller **Proof Reading: a.**"When will tea be ready?" asked Jim. **b.** "Do you want to go swimming with me?" **c.**"There is a lot of homework tonight!" cried Josie. **d.**It was nearly dark when mum called everyone, "Come to dinner!" **Punctuation:** The shepherd played silly pranks on other shepherds. They were very cross with him and I think I would be too. What do you think? **Volume:1a.**60cm^3 **b.**72cm^3 **c.**60cm^3 **2a.**4x2x2=16 **b.**5x2x3=30 **Chance:1a.**parent **2a.**1/4 **b.**1/5 **c.**1/8 **d.**1/10 **e.**1/3 **f.**1/8 **3a.**possible **b.**impossible **c.**possible
Unit 20	**Understanding:** Shade **a.**1 **b.**2 **c.**3 **d.**2 **Interpreting: a.**They should be able to assist and support others in the group. **b.**They work together to achieve the purpose and goals of the group. **c.**The leader needs to get on with all members in the group, be fair and give everyone a go. **d.** To do most of the difficult work. **Grammar:** Cross out -**a.**were, were **b.**was, was **c.**was, was **Correct verbs: a.**were, was **b.**were, was **c.** were **Word Building: a.** serve **b.** group **c.** head **d.** weaknesses **e.** share **f.** aims **Spelling: a.** knives **b.** wives **c.** lives **d.** wolves **e.** shelves **f.** halves **g.** loaves **h.** thieves **i.** leaves **a.**roofs **b.**dwarfs **c.**chefs **Proof Reading: a.**wolves **b.** roofs **c.**dwarfs **d.**wives **Punctuation:** 1914-1918; 1939-1945; May-June; August-September **Factors:1a.**42 **b.**32 **c.**24 **d.**35 **e.**54 **f.**24 **g.**56 **h.**33 **2a.**T **b.**T **c.**F **d.**T **e.**F **f.**T **Multiplication: 1a.**1 068 **b.**981 **c.**504 **d.**928 **e.**685 **f.**2 430 **2a.**80, 72, 48, 100, 40, 60 **b.**48, 16, 56, 64, 32, 40, 24, 72 **3a.**1L 500mL

Answers

Unit 21	**Understanding:** a.German b.French & Italian c. Merci d.French e.Friend **Interpreting:** a. danke b. good bye c.merci beaucoup d.gutten morgan e. Arrivederci Roma **Grammar:** a. before school/to the butchers b. after recess/to farewell Year 6 c. by lunch time d. In the afternoon/on the bus e. this evening/at the hall/over the river **Word Building:** a.progression b. multiplication c.division d.tension e. exploration f. decision **Spelling:** a. with eight tentacles b. eight notes in the range c. eighty years old d. eight sided shape e.Because the Julian Calendar (after Julius Caesar) began in March and count forward from there October is the eighth month. The current calendar is the Gregorian Calendar named after Pope Gregory. **AO:** occult, ochre octagon, octet octave, October, octogenarian, octopus **Punctuation:** a. ... red, brown, green … b. … cakes, fruits, lollies,… yes, c. …tomorrow, written… d. …. toys, food, gifts, … e. … trip, Turkey, Greece, Italy, Germany, Austria **Using a Calculator:** 1a.50 b.97 c.78 2a.71 b.123 c.125 d.175 3a.448, 1792 b.80,106 c.16, 8 **Addition:** 1a.$61.90 b.$146.95 c.$230.24 2.$265.10 3a.2,1 b.4,9 c.5,3
Unit 22	**Understanding:** Order –g,d,b,e,c,h,f,a **Interpreting:** a.No b.parent c.Yes d.Yes e.Yes **Grammar:** a. were racing b.are singing c.am going d.was helping e.are singing **Word Building:** parent **Spelling:** a. bow b.fare c.tear d.bow e.fare f.tear **Missing Letters:** a. chocolate b.slivered c.tablespoon d.container e.air tight f.vegetable g.vowels **Punctuation:** a. "Hurry up!" cried dad. b.The teacher asked, "has everyone finished?" c. "I will be late," said Dom. "So don't wait up." d."Why has the bell rung early?" asked Najib **Area:** 1a.ha b.km^2 2a.100 b.3 000m^2 c.80 d.9 3a.P=22cm A=2 000m^2 b.P=290m A=3 200m^2 **Subtraction:** 1a.5 312 b.4 422 c.2 251 d.6 314 e.7 315 f.4 149 2.959 3a.7,8 b.2,3 c.2,1
Unit 23	**Understanding:** a. Reading and Writing b.They usually manage by getting someone to do things requiring reading and writing for them. c.To have a knowledge and understanding of a required language. d.Without reading it is impossible to understand or be independently involved in day-to-day living activities. e. Without the basic skills it is hard to get a good job, earn good money, enjoy a quality lifestyle and participate fully in society. **Interpreting:** a.unable to do many things b.to spread information to others c.not able to do something d.how to put basic things together e.organisations funded by government usually, to give or lend a hand to those in need f. medicare, Centrelink, Defence, Education, Health … **Grammar:** a.We b.them c.She d.It e.They **Word Building:** parent **Spelling:** parent check **Dictionary Practice:** a. before b. after c. after d. before e. before f. after g. after h. after **Punctuation:** a. The storm came in quickly from the west and created havoc. b.They were waiting for a long time before they could move and take cover. **Time:** 1a.20:00 b.18:55 c.12:57 d.14:28 e.23:45 2a.seven thirty b.two twenty-five c.four fifteen d.eleven forty-five e.one minute past twelve OR one minute past midnight **Multiplication:** 1a.918 b.1 104 c.1 512 d.1 875 2 **Across** -1.72, 3.81, 5.44 6.35, 9.32, 11.308 **Down** -1.72, 2.14, 4.18, 6.32, 7.63, 8.30, 10.28
Unit 24	**Understanding:** a.T b.T c.T d.T e.T **Interpreting:** a.teachers/parents/principals b. Because of the information in the web address. c.The person who publishes the book at huntereducationnightingale. d.www.huntereducationnightingale.com.au e.9 **Grammar:** a.enjoyment b. amusement c.pleasant d.laughter e.delightful f.irritation **Word Building:** parent **Spelling:** gnarled, gnat, gnaw, gnome, honest, honorary, honour, honourable, knave, knead, knife, knight, know **Proof Reading:** Circle a. passed,damage, buildings b. When, stopped, flooded **Punctuation:** a. It is b. We are c. They are d. You will e. should have f. will not **Calculator:** a. 12 396, 37 188, 111 564 b. 58 413, 58 420, 58 427 c. 625, 390 625, 1 525 880 000 d. 10 663, 14 479 e. 7 684, 7337, 6 990 f. 13.28, 1.328, 0.1328 2. 111, 120, 360, 40, 20, 480, 50, 25 3a. 9.72 b. 14.24 c. 3.228 d. 0.38 e. 7.064 f. 1.132 **Equivalent Fractions:** 1.a. 2/10 b. 25 c. 0.2 d. 6.0 e. 3/4 f. 3/8 2a. 25% b. 4/10 c. 1/3 d. 0.5 e. 75% f. 4/5 3a. 2/4 b. 8/10 c. 3/5
Unit 25	**Understanding:** Shade a.3 b.2 c.3 d.1 **Interpreting:** a. The options for ways to pay have increased. b. For one week c.www.surfrider.com.au d. Monday to Sunday from 8:30am to 7:00pm e. A credit card uses the providers money until you pay for it but a debit card must have the money loaded on it in order for you to buy an item. **Grammar:** a. She will ring every night… b. The children will fall into the water. c. I will grow a new rose… d. He will come home late … **Spelling:** Circle a.threw b.flour c.reign d.sight e.light f.sole g.sure h.their/there **AO:** artist, chemist, dentist, florist, geologist, organist, pianist, prosthetist, soloist, typist **Punctuation:** a. We went to town for lunch, to shop and to buy shoes. b. Before long it was raining so we looked for shelter but couldn't find any. **Mass:** 1.cow-300kg, boy-45kg, pumpkin-5kg, book-2kg, apple-275g, cat-3kg, car-2T, pencil-10g, 2a.3kg b.4 ½ kg c.10kg 200g d.6 ½ kg e.8 ½ kg f.10 ¼ kg **Division:** 1a.T b.T c.F d.T e.f f.f 2a.120r7 b.223r1 c.125r2 d.170r3 e.71r1 f.121r4 3a.85 b.82
Unit 26	**Understanding: Shade** a. 2 b.4 c. 3 d. 3 **Interpreting:** a. What would have been worse for mum to pick up? b.Why was mum so distracted while serving dinner? c.What is asked of the reader? OR Who makes these sounds? d. What are you asked to do? e. Explain the meaning of each phrase. **Grammar:** a. over there, on the table b. outside the fence, near the road c. above ground, between the house and shed d. into the dam, near our house e. inside the hall **Word Building:** a. semitrailer b. semibreve c. semitone d. semidetached e. semicolon f. semicircle **Spelling:** half a sphere, hemispherical **Word Meanings:** a. lingering b. attribute c.dulcet d.distract e.concentrate f. compromise **Punctuation:** a. Dr and Mrs Dib are coming to Christmas Carols in the park. b. The new principal is Mr Abdul and the new teacher will be Mrs Shahidi. c. Paul and Josie share the same birthday, 1 September. d. Matthew and Patrick are brothers and Sam and Valentina are their brother and sister. **Credit Card:** 1 Might include; food, clothing, petrol, meals, theme park tickets, On-line goods and so on… 2a.7539 1234 5678 4321 b. MyBank c. Ms G M I Good d. Wireless or WiFi e. 08/20 **Money:** 1 colour = a,b,e,g 2a.$8 b.$4.50 c.$12 d.$1.80

Answers

Unit 27	**Understanding:** a. No b.Yes c. No d.Yes e.Yes f.Yes g.Yes h.Yes **Interpreting:** Tick all items **Grammar:** Underline: a. icy, cold deserts; hot, dry desert b. rocky deserts, large plants, enormous areas of hot, dry land c.The Kalahari Desert, the Simpson Desert, hot, dry days and cold nights d. Extreme heat, freezing cold, World deserts e. Dry soil, high humidity, very little precipitation, harsh and dangerous places. **Word Building:** a. subway b. subject c. submerge d. sublime e. submariner f. subscription g. subsequent h.subterranean i. subdivide **Spelling:** a.one thing or another. Parent b. temperature Parent c. a ram Parent **Syllabification:** a. e/vap/or/a/tion b. ve/ge/ta/tion c. pre/cip/i/ta/tion d. tem/per/a/ture e. kil/om/et/re f. A/rab/i/an g. Kal/a/har/i h. Mon/go/li/a **Punctuation:** a. ! b.? c. ? d. Run, Tom! e. "Are you wet?" he asked. **Circles:** 1a.10mm b.15mm c.20mm 2a.60mm b.30mm c.40mm **3D Objects:** 1. Square Pyramid 2. Cone 3. hexagonal prism 4. cylinder 5. hexagonal pyramid 6. cube
Unit 28	**Understanding:** Tick a, b, c, d, f, g, h, i, j **Interpreting:** a. To listen to the sounds and enjoy the sights. b. For thousands of years c. Rock formations in Central Australia d. A corroboree OR Initiation ceremonies e. Alice Springs **Grammar:** a. underline: is Subject: Uluru-Kata-Tjuta National Park b. underline: perform Subject: The local tribe c. underline:formed Subject: The Olgas and Uluru d.underline: has easy walking Subject: The Valley of the Winds e. underline: can still enjoy Subject: Disabled or elderly visitors **Word Building:** a. M b. M c. M d. F e. C f. C g. F h. F i. C j. N **Spelling:** a.to, two b. too, to, two c. two, two, to d. two, two, too **Proof Reading:** a. No doubt he knows the right way to swim. b. Their books will be ready when he is. c. Those cows are too sick to move. d. Suddenly the ground opened up. **Punctuation:** a. JP b. MC c. s-s-w d. Mr and Mrs Fahmi went to see Madam Butterfly at the Sydney Opera House. **Faces and Nets:** 1 match- a-g, b-f, c-h, d-e **Location:** . 
Unit 29	**Understanding:** Tick a, b, c **Interpreting:** a. happening yearly b. always, forever c. greeted d. items brought for holiday camping e. appealing to look at f. not necessary to say g. seeing in a clear light h. satisfied, certain i. commemorate an event j. known or seen **Grammar:** a. we are b. they are or they were a. they will d. we will e. it is f. is not g. there will h. who will i. we have j. shall not k. would have l. must have **Word Building:** parent check
Unit 30	**Revision:** Parent check correct spelling **AO:** a. author b. conductor c. doctor d. governor e. inspector f. navigator g. sailor h. sculptor i. tailor **Punctuation:** a. "I will be ready by two o'clock Jane, but I can't get a bus until two-thirty." b. "Why is the game so early?" cried dad. "I won't be ready at that time." c. "Does he know where to put the new furniture when it is delivered?" mum asked "Or will it be left outside?" **Location:** 1.Samson Sports Ground 2.Post Office 3.Golf Club 4.P12-13 5.Underpass 6.N-S 7.NE 8.J1-2 9.Hospital 10.E-W 11.North 12.Car Park